# Trail's End

## The Mike Isnardy Story

*In Appreciation*
*Judy Alsager*

# By Judy Alsager

ISBN 0-9682883-2-4
Copyright © 2005 Judy Alsager

First Edition 2005

Cover photo by Patrick Hattenberger
Sonny DeRose on Ol' Come Apart

Published in Canada by
**Bluedoor** Box 4563
—*publishing*— Williams Lake, B.C.
Fax/Phone: 250-747-8402

For Mike...

> 'Let us return to the past
> and that will be progress'...

— Guiseppe Verdi, composer

Mike Isnardy

# Contents

# Acknowledgments —————

I wish to thank Mike for opening the door of his very eventful life to me.

Many others contributed to the process of finally bringing this manuscript to completion:

Thanks to:
Mike's family and friends – in particular Amedee and Alice; Richard Dick; Willy and Terry Crosina, thanks for your good memories. Also to Hank and Julie Krynen, Lenny and Cecilia DeRose, and countless important others who provided stories, pictures, map searching, etc.

Paul Meyer, of Zebron Productions, New Westminster, B.C., for ongoing professional advice and support.

Layout and Design: Cheryl Bailey

The Archives Section of the Williams Lake Library.

# Preface

Rodeo is probably the most popular sport in the province of British Columbia. The thrill of the competition, the glamour and the romance; the visiting, camaraderie, and always that unforgettable riding or roping feat that will forever be remembered and talked about in rodeo circles – participants and fans travel many a gruelling mile to attend the various rodeos throughout the area.

Local cowboy/rancher Mike Isnardy was a cornerstone in the foundation of rodeo organization in B.C. That was not his intention in the beginning. In 1960, he simply started some recreation roping and bronc riding in his corral with a few friends on leisurely Sunday afternoons. By 1965, it had advanced to be the Interior Amateur Rodeo Association;  and from there, it just grew, and grew, and grew...

Mike followed his passion for buying and bartering for quality bucking horses – before long his famous bucking string was sought after by rodeo events throughout the province. The notorious Ol' Come-Apart, whose record for throwing riders was unsurpassed, drew crowds from near and far. Many of Mike's buckers are still entertaining cheering crowds of rodeo fans today.

All this created a web that connected all the rodeos together and resulted, in 1988, in them all being governed by one strong organization called the British Columbia Rodeo Association. A non-profit amateur/semi-pro association, it keeps rodeo at the top of the list for crowd-pleasing and tourist-drawing entertainment.

In 2001, Mike Isnardy was inducted into the B.C. Cowboy Hall of Fame for his passionate contribution to the formation of this all-important Rodeo Association.

# Introduction

I first met Mike Isnardy in the early spring of 1980. I lived at Bear Springs, a remote area six miles towards the back country from the main yard of the famous Gang Ranch, which my family owned at that time, in the central Cariboo area of British Columbia.

It was springtime, and the steep road to Bear Springs was muddy – not many had dared to travel it lately, and I was surprised to see a van-type of vehicle in the yard. A youthful looking man in a wheelchair had already commandeered my small children to help him push himself across the lumpy ground towards the hayfield where the buffalo herd was grazing, their reddish newborn calves bouncing around in the sunshine with their tails in the air.

I looked for the people who had brought him, and couldn't find anyone. He had come alone. This was my first hint at his fearlessness.

The visitor was Mike Isnardy, and his first words to me were, "I've waited a long time to see a buffalo up close." He acted as though he wasn't even in a wheelchair as he tried to get as close to the huge animals as he could. Amazingly, they didn't seem to mind his intrusion on their maternal duties.

As we visited over lunch, we got our first glimpse of a resilient and capable horseman and rancher. Quiet and gentlemanly, he gave us tidbits of his past, which proved to be as fascinating as his present. I knew this man had many stories, and a colorful life.

I have developed a phobia, a fear of losing these people from this hardworking, slower simpler era. It's not just Mike Isnardy, it's all the "workers of the earth" from that entire generation who expended so much energy for so little return; who would rather die than be dishonest; their principles and thought processes geared to the responsibilities and integrity of a lifestyle that made so much more sense than the fast-whirling computerized electronic driven society we have now created.

I don't think they can be replaced, and I can't imagine what kind of world we will be left with when they leave us, one by precious one, and take with them their work ethics, their ruggedness and abilities, their good-natured humour, and their unbelievable stories.

This book is my attempt to keep at least some of their stories alive. Maybe, just maybe, it can offer a brief but welcome escape back to a slower simpler lifetime.

Judy Alsager, Author

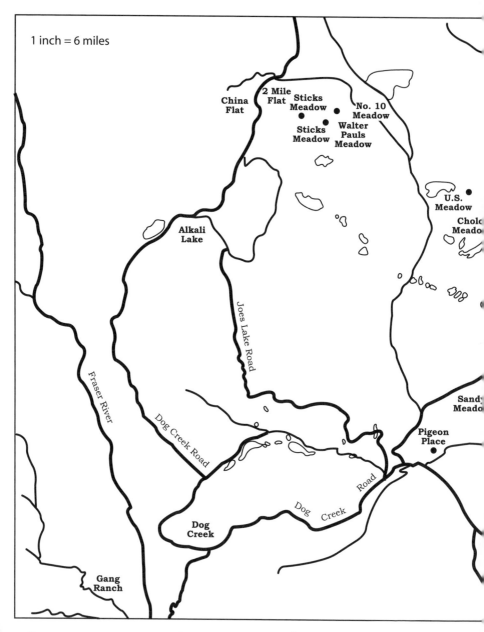

1 inch = 6 miles

China Flat

2 Mile Flat

Sticks Meadow

Sticks Meadow

No. 10 Meadow

Walter Pauls Meadow

U.S. Meadow

Chol Meado

Alkali Lake

Joes Lake Road

Fraser River

Dog Creek Road

Sand Meado

Pigeon Place

Dog Creek Road

Dog Creek

Dog Creek

Gang Ranch

Springhouse and Surrounding Area

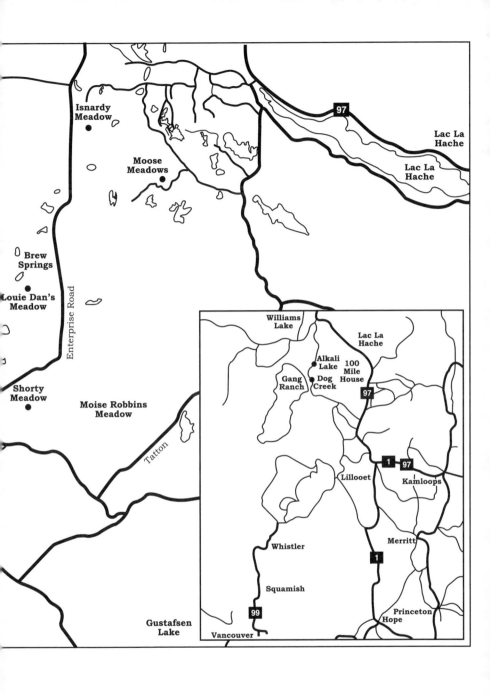

# Isnardy Family Tree

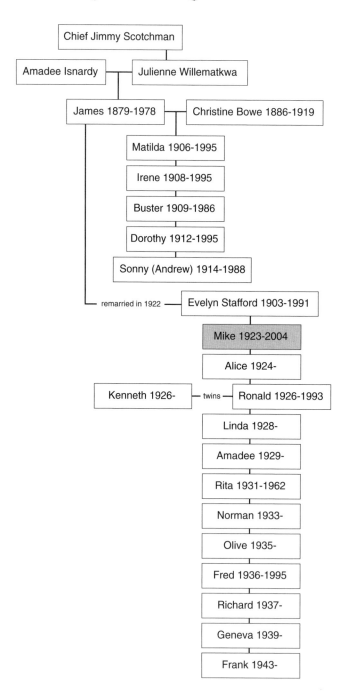

Chief Jimmy Scotchman

Amadee Isnardy — Julienne Willematkwa

James 1879-1978 — Christine Bowe 1886-1919

Matilda 1906-1995

Irene 1908-1995

Buster 1909-1986

Dorothy 1912-1995

Sonny (Andrew) 1914-1988

remarried in 1922 — Evelyn Stafford 1903-1991

Mike 1923-2004

Alice 1924-

Kenneth 1926- — twins — Ronald 1926-1993

Linda 1928-

Amadee 1929-

Rita 1931-1962

Norman 1933-

Olive 1935-

Fred 1936-1995

Richard 1937-

Geneva 1939-

Frank 1943-

# Where it all Began

## Chapter 1

Irish Tom was not a pretty horse. An almost dung-colored mangy-maned sorrel, he came from the Merritt, B.C. area; owned and later sold by Jack Moffatt, who operated a local tavern there. Jack claimed that Irish Tom had once made his mark as a racehorse.

Whatever glories had touched him in the past were long gone, Irish Tom was now an unwilling farm horse – a powerhouse of unleashed fury and quivering horse muscle. He was not at all in favor of the stubborn man-flesh that had now settled confidently into the wellworn saddle on his back, nor the unfamiliar wide belt that was cinched so tightly around his girth – his flaring nostrils caught a familiar man scent – a smell that initiated bad memories for Irish Tom.

For a moment he paused, as though giving the man one last chance to change his mind and leap off. Snorting and rolling his eyes backwards as best he could towards the intruder on his back, he realized this was not going to happen – in fact, the cowboy's legs were tightening firmly around Irish Tom's rib cage, readying for the explosion he could feel building between his thighs and knees. Lowering his head and flattening his ears, and giving a few straight-legged hops, the horse gave the rider yet more opportunity to get off before bursting into wholehearted open warfare.

Twisting and bucking, rotating in circles, then changing directions, Irish Tom vented every effort into throwing off this rider. The man hung on doggedly - as much as this pounding fury beneath him wanted rid of him, he was determined to stay on. Round and round, a crazed violent dance of sorts, to a background of leather-slapping noises, grunts and his own rasping sounds from the breath being jerked through his tightly clenched teeth, the cowboy tried to anticipate the horse's next move, and match his own movements to them.

The battle raged on and on, a personal test of strengths involving no-one except the man and the horse – a contest of wills that would ultimately produce just one winner. It escalated into a blurry dust cloud that travelled across the yard in the direction of the log barn.

At long last, Irish Tom's rage was spent – he tired of this battle; with the loss of his energy came the realization that he could not separate this rider from him. Offering a few more parting spasms, he finally stood still, legs apart, head down, panting, accepting.

The cowboy in the saddle partially relaxed his grip and sat quietly amidst the settling dust, giving the horse a chance to adjust to this new dimension of his life – the first step towards developing a relationship of respect and teamwork with a human. He knew from experience that his work was not done with this horse – the first major furrow had been made, now the seeds of trust and respect needed to be planted in a continuous and never-faltering manner.

Halfway across the yard towards the weathered log dwelling, the man's young son crouched behind the safety of a wooden wagon, his bare toes curled tensely in the dust, his fingers tightly clenched around the top of the wheel as he peered wide-eyed through the spokes.

He watched, transfixed, in awe of the man who had just conquered the frothing horse.

Even his father didn't realize the impact this had on the young boy – and how this event would instill in four-year-old Mike Isnardy's mind a lifelong fascination for bucking horses, and an undying respect for the heroism of the staunch men who climbed fearlessly onto their backs.

The broncbuster was James Isnardy and, although this 1927 spring morning's interlude with Irish Tom was to be of lasting memorable importance to his son, Mike, it was merely a routine task in the activities of a normal day for James. This was just one of many untamed horses that required "breaking" before the working season began.

James's descendants were of hardy stock – his father Amedee Isnardy was born in 1840 in Nice, France. At only fourteen years of age, he and his two brothers stowed away on a boat heading for Mexico. From there, the enterprising teenager worked his way up to California, and then eventually up to British Columbia around 1859, no doubt following alluring stories of lush goldfields.

Following the Harrison route to Lillooet, he operated a store there for a few years, where he met and married an Indian princess – Julienne Willematkwa, the daughter of Chief Jimmy Scotchman of the Lillooet area. 1862 found them on the move again, ending up in the Chimney Creek area south of Williams Lake in the interior of B.C., where land was available for pre-empting.

Chimney Creek was so named, as in 1842 Father Modeste Demers, the first missionary to travel to the interior of British Columbia, visited the Indian village of Shuswaps on the banks of the Fraser River. A priest's hut and church with a rough stone chimney was built for him. The nearby creek was named "Chimney Creek".

The Chimney Creek area was a vast treed plateau above and following alongside the mighty Fraser River. Trembling aspen bushes surrounded bunchgrass meadows where plentiful wildlife enjoyed shelter and abundant feed. There was poplar, spruce and lodgepole pine readily available for use in building and construction of the houses and outbuildings that these early settlers needed.

Amadee and Julienne settled happily and enthusiastically on their pre-emption land; they were tired of moving and travelling, and were ready to settle down and throw all their energies into their homestead.

This signified the beginning of one of the largest family trees in the Cariboo – eventually including family names of Tressiera, Stafford, Grinder, English, Pinchbeck, Bowe and more. Amedee was a hardworking and energetic man, who soon was acquiring more land – his huge ranch would grow to stretch all the way from the Fraser River up the Chimney Creek Valley to Brunson Lake beyond.

Amedee Isnardy laid claim to the oldest water rights in the Cariboo. In order to irrigate his farmlands, he hired fifty Chinese, paying them each fifty cents per day. These industrious workers, with picks and shovels, built a system of ditches along the valley which can still be seen today parallel to Chimney Lake Road. Many of the Chinese were buried on the Ranch, but in later years the bodies were dug up and shipped back to their homeland of China.

As is the case with any river, there always seemed to be a need for people to cross to the other side. Canoes would cross the Fraser, continually searching for the best spot where the current wasn't so strong. At times they balanced carriages on top of the canoes and carefully shuttled them across, their wheels removed and placed inside, and the horses tied on behind. It was always a harrowing and dangerous experience, and a relief to reach the opposite shore.

Amedee started a ferry system across the Fraser River, to shuttle people and goods to and from the Chilcotin territory which lay west of the Fraser River. His son Joe later took this over, as Amedee turned his attention to the business of shaping up his homestead. He struck up a lasting friendship with a Hudson Bay packer by the name of Cataline, who pastured his mules along the Fraser River between Dog Creek and Alkali, the area neighbouring Amedee's homestead.

Cataline was a wild sort, a long-haired driver of mule trains who was known to drink rum and to soak his long hair with it. He would take a bath in the snow when the necessity and the urge hit him. No-one ever knew where he would show up next. His packing expeditions using his countless mule teams took him to regions near and far, and he grew to speak a language all his own – French, Spanish, English, Chinese, Shuswap, and a little Mexican thrown in. Gradually he cut back on his mule trains, and by 1910 he was reduced to two mule trains of approximately seventy-five head each. Amadee kept watch over his livestock when Cataline was away on his excursions.

James Isnardy was born to Amedee and Julienne in Chimney Creek in 1879. Hardworking and tough, the family embedded itself in the toil and purpose of establishing themselves at Springhouse, outside of Williams Lake in the interior of the Cariboo Chilcotin area of B.C. – raising cattle and horses, farming and operating sawmills. They survived and thrived, extending their family to become an integral part of the community, and remain so to this very day.

James was raised in this hardworking environment. Although he was a capable handler of all manner of livestock, and a tough outdoorsman, he also played the violin.

James grew up and married Christine, a wholesome twenty-year-old girl from the local established Bowe family. Children followed in succession – Tillie (Matilda) in 1906, Irene (Curly) in 1908, James (Buster) in 1909, Dorothy in 1912, and Andrew (Sonny) in 1914. Sadly this busy mother Christine, died in 1919 at the young age of thirty-three leaving James, at the age of forty, with five children to care for, the oldest one being early teens, the youngest one five.

Three years later, in October of 1922, James married again – to Evelyn Stafford, a stalwart young lady from England. She was the oldest of five children in the homesteading Stafford family that had come to the area from the lower mainland area of B.C. with another family by the name of Petrowitz. The Staffords had immigrated from England when Evelyn was but three years old.

Evelyn was nineteen when she married James Isnardy in 1922. He was forty-three, with five motherless children, some of them almost her own age. Where any other young woman might have seen this situation as a mountain too high to climb, Evelyn threw herself into the midst of the maelstrom. She was capable and hard-working, and obviously fearless. She had already been caring for brothers and sisters born after her in the Stafford family. She was used to this kind of life.

One year later, in 1923, Mike was born to James and Evelyn; twelve more children would follow after him over the next twenty years, and he already had five older siblings from the previous marriage of James and Christine.

The childbirth process was very much a family affair. All of the babies were born at home, with the exception of the last two, Frank and Geneva.

Mike Isnardy was born in their old log house at Chimney Creek. A company called Avery and Pigeon (A&P), a logging and ranching partnership, owned this place. A year after Mike was born, a little sister, Alice, was delivered by her father.

With five older brothers and sisters, and twelve more to follow after him, Mike was introduced to a world of unending chores and uncomplaining acceptance of a home filled to capacity with other bodies, all of which had various needs and requirements. He learned to share everything he had, unselfishly, as they all did. Mike took his first uncertain steps in the same well-worn leather baby boots that had been carefully wrapped in paper and stored away after each of his five older brothers and sisters had learned to walk in them. When Mike's growing toes pushed at the ends of these shoes, they were again stowed away until his sister Alice was born a year later. If any of the children could not fit into a pair of shoes that were handed down from their older siblings, they went barefoot. Scraps of leather were never discarded, as they were used to repair or patch any footwear that started to fall apart, or fashion a new sole for a worn boot.

When Mike was two, the family moved to Long Lake at Springhouse Trails, this was a larger house that they rented from a man by the name of George Gill. There was an upstairs in this house, and two bedrooms – James and Evelyn had one bedroom, with two home-made cribs in it. The newest baby and the next youngest slept in this bedroom with their parents. The other children shared the remaining bedroom, girls on one side, boys on the other.

Within a year of this move, twins Ronald and Kenneth were born, again delivered by their father. This time James called upon Evelyn's mother, Granny Stafford, to help, as Evelyn was quite certain about the fact that she felt the movements of two growing bodies within her over-sized belly. Mike's Aunt Hortence from Peevine also showed up to assist. A lengthy labor finally produced a gratifying wail from newborn Kenneth, followed shortly by his brother Ronald. There was much scurrying around the busy household, as the necessary duties for the newborns and their exhausted mother were doubled.

The birth of the twin boys caused much excitement for the older children, who found more opportunities to hold the new babies, being as there were two of them. Mike was three years old and Alice was just two – although Matilda, Irene and Buster had already left home, fourteen-year-old Dorothy and twelve-year-old Sonny were often recruited to help out with the growing number of toddlers.

The ongoing commotion proved a bit much for Mike. At the very young age of three, he spent a good deal of his time outdoors where he was not in the way, forming alliances with every animal he could make acquaintance with. Horses were an inborn favorite for him. With that many children in a family, he never even thought of asking anyone to take time to lift him up onto a horse. He learned that he could take a handful of hay, put it on the ground in front of the horse, and when the horse bent his head down to the hay, Mike was quick to climb onto the solid and powerful neck – there he would sit and wait patiently until the horse raised his head again, this upward movement would slide him down the horses neck onto his back. He always rode bareback.

To harness the workhorses, he would climb up on a fence with the harness so that he could reach to fit the large work halters over their heads, and the cumbersome harness over their broad backs. He had watched his father do this many times, and was quick to learn the buckles and snaps routine that was required to hold everything in place.

He rode on one of the milk cows, a gentle Jersey-Hereford cross, to bring the others home at milking time. He would give each cow a portion of grain so that she would stand still and eat contentedly while being milked. Cows could rather miraculously "chew their cud" after the feed was all gone. They would regurgitate already-swallowed feed to be rechewed and enjoyed all over again.

Mike then hunkered down on his haunches beside the bulging udder and squeezed warm streams of milk into a pail held securely between his knees to ensure the cow didn't kick it over. He tucked the cow's tail tight behind his bent knee, so that when the cow swatted at flies, he wouldn't be the target of her rope-like smackings. He had already been taught to check the teats for any sores or open cuts, as the cow was sure to kick if a painful teat was squeezed. The milking had to be done punctually twice a day to avoid an engorged and painful udder.

The cats would always be in the barn at milking time, standing close enough with their mouths wide open, so that the warm milk could be squirted straight into their gaping throats, direct from the cow's teats. Afterwards they would lick any remnants from their whiskers and fur. Sometimes the kids who were milking the cows would squirt each other, making sure they didn't get caught wasting the milk in this fashion. After they were milked, the cows were turned out to pasture again, and the kids shared the other chores of feeding and watering the chickens, pigs, horses and sheep. James had thoroughly instilled in his children's minds the importance of looking after all the animals before their own needs were considered. This would become a lifelong habit.

There was no television for entertainment – neither

were there videos, computers, stereos or radios, or telephones. Their times for relaxation were spent with their animals. A favorite past-time was to teach tricks to the various dogs and cats that were always prevalent – lining them up on chairs or bales and training them to do all kinds of antics. His father would place the chairs three or four feet apart, then teach the dogs to jump back and forth. He would then advance them to jump over his back, then through a circle he made with his arms. Even Poogo the tom cat learned to master these tricks. James would be sure to reward them with some kind of treat after they performed.

Life became a challenging succession of moving to bigger houses, where there was work to support this family and space to raise the animals and feed required to subsist. Work was never-ending, and the children born into this family with such regularity were moulded automatically into the never-ending tasks that evolved from keeping the farm going. Chores were a normal and accepted part of their lives, what with caring for the younger ones, feeding the ever-hungry family, and eventually working off the farm for others.

James Isnardy, Mike's father        Evelyn Stafford, Mike's mother

Mike's older siblings: Dorothy, Irene (Curly), James (Buster), Sonny
& Matilda (Tillie) Chimney Creek, where Mike was born

# On the Move

## Chapter 2

"Everybody pack up," Mike's father called out, as he maneuvered the team with the wagon as close to the door of the house as possible. Five-year-old Mike knew that when the horses brought that big wagon and parked at the house that it was moving time again. The kids were used to this routine, they began piling belongings in the wagon, from outside and inside. Nothing could be left behind, as everything they owned was an essential item. They must remember the axes and wedges (used to fit into a crack made in a stubborn piece of wood to facilitate splitting when hit with the axe) from the woodshed; the pails, forks, bridles, halters and ropes from the barn; all the heavy items on the bottom; blankets and bedding and kitchen paraphernalia on the top.

Some of the family would go the new place first, to organize things in the house as they were brought. The last load hauled the people who were left, and the cats and dogs. Livestock was driven or ridden to the new farm. Mike and the others threw themselves into the business of relocating – it was exciting – different house, new neighbours, greener pastures, change of scenery. It was an adventure, new trails to be ridden, unfamiliar territory to be explored, unwary woodchucks and grouse to be hunted. At this time there were ten children, and a roomier house was welcome, if not essential. They left the old house and its memories happily, and, after some jostling and rearranging, snugly fit into their new surroundings. It was out of the question for anyone to expect their own room, or even shared rooms. It was more like a barracks with beds wall-to-wall.

This move was to Rose Place, just a half a mile west. It was named after Fred Rose, today the Herrick family lives there. The family could let out its seams a little.

The Hereford-cross milk cow had a new calf. Mike's Dad had put the new calf in the pen by the barn with its mother. Five-year-old Mike spent time with the little whitefaced newcomer, making friends, letting it suck on his fingers through the fence.

Soon he decided to climb into the pen and get closer to his newfound buddy, as the mother cow was busy in the corner concentrating on pulling away at a pile of hay with her tongue. The calf was certainly receptive to this, standing there rubbing his head on Mike while he got his neck scratched and petted. Mike knelt down on his knees, giggling as the calf made funny movements with his head and butted playfully at Mike.

Suddenly Mike felt a movement behind him. Starting to turn, he realized the angry cow was almost on top of him, chasing him away from her calf. Not even having time to stand up before she got to him, Mike scrambled away on his knees, crawling as fast as he could as she tried to bunt him and hook him with her horn. Lunging towards the fence, Mike squeezed underneath to the safety of the other side, as the cow stood huffing and pawing at him from the pen. Mike looked up to see his father leaning over the fence, laughing at the excitement and remarking that he had never seen anyone crawl that fast.

New places also brought new perils. There was a granary in the yard that was used to store the all-important feed grain for the animals. One night either the latch on the door was not fastened properly, or some clever horse managed to nudge it open. By the time it was noticed that four horses were inside the granary, they had managed to gorge themselves with as much grain as possible. Not only had they managed to get into the granary, but somehow had maneuvered the door to close behind them, so that it was some time before anyone noticed they were happily locked in with all the grain they could greedily consume.

This resulted in a very dangerous colicky condition in the horses called foundering – caused by a bloating gas build-up in the stomach from overeating grain. When the horses were found in the granary, Mike's dad hurried to get help to walk them. It was important not to allow them to roll or lie down. Round and round they were forced to follow those who tirelessly kept them moving, their distended stomachs adding to their extreme discomfort. When one person tired of marching them in circles, someone else took over. An intensely high fever affected their hooves – the hooves actually became hot and very sore, especially in the front part. Two of the horses died, the others managed to be saved, but were left lame.

In addition to trying to save the horses, the normal everyday chores had to be carried out. Feeding and milking could not be put off until "later". Every member of the family was part of the work detail needed to accomplish this.

The Isnardy family was now supplying milk, eggs, cream, vegetables, chickens, pigs, and sheep to Williams Lake. Once a week the delivery wagon made the scheduled trip to Williams Lake with the proceeds of a week's toiling on the farm. The milk and cream had to be kept cool in the summer so that it wouldn't sour before it got to its destination. In summer, the milk was hung from a rope down into the coolness of the well. Later they constructed an "ice house" – where they used ice blocks cut from the lake. Sawdust was used to insulate the ice from melting; logs framed the outside walls. Butter, milk, eggs and cream could be stored properly. The trip to town was commenced very early in the morning, to avoid the summer mid-day heat. The cream was shipped on to Quesnel by train. Vegetables had to be delivered while they were fresh. Eggs were sold, forty-eight dozen a week.

In winter, everything was reversed – the produce, eggs and dairy products had to be kept from freezing. The trip was made after the sun came up, to take advantage of any amount of added warmth. Rocks were heated, wrapped in sacks, and placed in the wagon to keep things from freezing. Proceeds from these transactions were used to purchase the list of items needed to be brought back to the farm – supplies that they couldn't grow – sugar, coffee, molasses, rice, peanut butter, flour, raisins, lamp oil, precious treats both needed and desired.

Trips to stores for shopping were an event – money was scarce, and most purchases were made from trading. Especially in the more remote areas west of Williams Lake, where the climate was not suitable for growing produce to barter, trading for furs was an established industry. This produced a particularly hardy population of settlers who survived by hunting and trapping. Prices paid for the furs ranged anywhere from twenty-five cents for a squirrel, to ten dollars for a prime coyote hide.

In 1928, another new baby wailed her way into the Isnardy clan – a sweet little girl called Linda. This prompted another move for the family – to the Lawrence Boitano Place at Springhouse, just one mile west of the Springhouse Church. The team pulled the big wagon up to the house again, and everyone once again flew into the moving mode.

The new house was made from logs, with a grass-topped roof of sod, and a wooden floor of 1" x 12" rough board lumber. The kids soon discovered the sod roof was a fun place to play, and chased each other around on top of the earthen layers, until they got into trouble for causing it to leak.

This time James and Ken had loaded up a ponderous roan cow from Bill Isnardy's in a wagon with four foot wooden sides. They had decided this was the easiest way to move her to the new homestead. The road was uphill, and as James slapped the reins on the team to make them pull harder up the steep grade, the wagon lurched and the cow stepped to one side in an effort to keep her balance. This tipped the wagon over, spilling out James, Ken and Mike, and of course the panic-stricken cow. She scrambled to her feet and bolted away from the upset wagon. Mike held onto the team while James and Ken chased after her. She was wild with fright, and every time they headed in her direction, she took off running in the opposite direction. Darkness would soon be upon them, and the horses were agitated, still hooked to the over-turned wagon.

There was nothing else to do but leave her there, to be retrieved later, when she was calmed down. They unhooked the team from the wagon, and headed them towards home, walking dejectedly behind. They kept looking back, hoping that the cow would follow them, but she had had her fill of all of them.

At first light the next morning, Mike and Ken rode their horses back to the scene of the upset, and found the cow calmly grazing in Archie Petrowitz's meadow. They tied ropes onto the overturned wagon, wrapped the other end around their saddle horns, then urged and kicked their horses until the forlorn-looking wagon was upturned. The cow, engrossed with pulling at the sweet meadow grass, barely objected as they looped the rope around her neck, tied her to the wagon, and led her home.

Mike and Ken were responsible for getting the fire going in the morning, to warm the house up for the girls to get up and begin making breakfast and lunches. Winter mornings were dark and cold; Mike and Ken made certain they had dry kindling and cut wood stored by the stove the night before, so they could get warmed up faster in the mornings. When the stove was crackling and promising to produce hot water in the side reservoir, they would head out to the barn to feed the animals and milk the cows. They knew that by the time they returned from these chores, there would be warm water to dip out into the wash basin for washing up, and sausages or bacon would be sizzling on the cookstove. The fresh milk they carried in would be poured through a strainer cloth before drinking; there would be hearty farm-sized eggs from the chickens, and a pot of porridge steaming alongside the simmering metal coffee pot.

Despite the number of family members, there was never a shortage of food – although there were many mouths to feed, there were also many hands to bake bread, plant gardens, pick berries, milk cows, and to raise all the meat and vegetables and dairy products they needed.

Moving was as simple as hitching up the team to the wagon, loading it up, and unloading it at the new place. It was about this time, in the early 1930's, that another local family found a novel way of moving. Texas Fosbery, whose family owned a place in the Big Creek area, and who grew up to lead a colorful life as bush pilot, cowboy and catskinner – was only seven when his parents decided to move the family from Ashcroft to the Okanagan area. They loaded two hundred head of cattle into rail cars and their five horses into a boxcar with their Model A vehicle, freight wagon, furniture, chickens, cats and dogs. Then, under the security of darkness in the middle of the night, Tex and his brother Tony were told to be very quiet and were packed into the boxcar by their parents. They were hurriedly stuffed into the Model A while their tent was rolled up and packed in behind them.

There were CPR police in those days to watch for people trying to get free rides on the trains, so they spent the night in the pitch dark, being absolutely quiet. Finally there was a big bang and a lurch, as their car was being hooked on to the train, and they were mobile, headed down the tracks until the next afternoon. The freight then had to go by barge from Vernon down through the Okanagan Valley, as the rail line ended. All the cars were pushed onto a barge by the engine. When they were safely away from the dock on this sternwheeler, Tex and his brother Tony were allowed out of the rail car.

Mike (back), Ken, Ron, Linda, Alice, Springhouse 1930s
Liz Twan photo

Richard Isnardy

On the Move

**"**Sit still, would ya?!" Mike admonished Kenny, as he slid the sharp haircutting scissors along the back of the three-year-old's neck to catch any stray areas he had missed. Kenny tried to quit squirming, but found it difficult to ignore the hungry mosquito that had discovered the scab on his skinned knee.

It was 1929, Mike was six years old and, although he should have been in school on this day, it was haying season. It was not always possible for the children to attend school in this crucial time when the precious feed stacks were being harvested for the animal's winter survival. Evelyn and James both needed to work in the hayfields. This meant that some of the schoolage children had to stay home to care for their preschool age siblings.

Today Mike was home caring for five-year-old Alice, three-year-old twins Kenny and Ronald, one-year-old Linda, and his newborn baby brother Amadee, just a few months old. Evelyn had nursed the new baby before she hurried off to help James with the hay sloop – he now slumbered contentedly in a cradle right in the middle of all the noise, tightly wrapped in a well-used baby blanket to make him feel secure.

Mike stood back and surveyed the rather erratic hairstyle he was performing on Kenny – no matter which side he went to, it didn't seem to match up to the length of the other side. He kept shortening one side, then the other, still it seemed uneven. Finally, he was snipping nearly on the top of Kenny's head.

"What the heck, it's summer – you'll be glad to be rid of it," he finally said to Kenny in exasperation. With that, he snipped all the hair off Kenny's head, as close to the scalp as he could cut. Now no-one had to worry whether it was even or not.

Kenny sat quite still now as Mike again stepped back to admire his handiwork. Now the eyebrows seemed too much, as the rest of the hair was gone.

"Close your eyes, Ken," Mike told him. He then advanced upon Kenny's squeezed-shut eyes with the scissors and snip-snipped away at the silky black eyelashes that fringed his eyelids. Kenny seemed to sense the seriousness of staying still for this exercise and sat rigid as a stone.

Now Mike got James' straight-bladed razor that sat in a cracked cup by the washbasin.

"Hold still a bit longer," he said to Kenny, "you look funny with those bushy eyebrows and nothing else!" He then used the razor to shave off the three-year-old's eyebrows.

Now when he stood back to observe, he couldn't hold back his laughter, at Kenny's bald head and now even balder looking eyes.

Suddenly a knock at the door interrupted the merriment. Four-year-old Alice dashed to open the door to find a policeman standing there.

Constable John Blatchford took in the scene, from the six-year-old wielding the scissors, to the strange-looking little boy sitting amidst a pile of hair, to the cute little girl who had answered the door, another small boy who looked very much like the one sitting on the table, except this one had hair. He saw a baby girl sitting on a blanket on the plank floor, surrounded by a wooden spoon and a tin cup and other toys; also what appeared to be a tiny baby blissfully asleep in a cradle in the middle of it all.

"Where are your parents?" he asked the strangely quiet group.

Mike pointed in the direction of the hayfield.

"How old are you?" asked the policeman, "Why aren't you in school? One of your neighbours has complained that some children in this family are staying out of school!"

Truancy was not tolerated, and the police were quick to respond to a situation such as this. After getting a promise from Mike that he would be in school tomorrow, he left, but not without a further warning, "I'll be checking on you!"

Mike headed off to Grade One at the the local country school. He drove the team and sleigh, taking feed along for the horses. There was a barn at the school , where the horses were kept during school hours. At their lunch break, any children with horses would see that they were watered, and clean out their stalls.

The Springhouse School was a one-room log building with a peaked roof located about a mile and a half from the Isnardy farm. It was constructed from logs by Charlie Harry and Ingvard Johnson, and chinked with mud and moss between the logs to keep the cold out and the heat in. When this school burnt to the ground after its first construction, it was quickly rebuilt again. The growing community wanted and needed a school, which became the hub of the district's social activities. Today it stands in reverence at the Springhouse Trails Ranch.

There were normally twelve or thirteen students in attendance at the little log house of learning - homespun-dressed children of the local families: the Staffords, Isnardys, Westwicks, Elliotts, Frizzi, Petrowitz. They brought their lunches of homemade bread with peanut butter, and apples, in syrup pails or lard buckets that served as lunch pails. An outside bell summoned the students to hurry up and present themselves to the school teacher inside.

Miss Winnifred Weetman was a brave teacher at the school, followed by Mr. Field.

Everyone was fully aware of the thick leather strap Mr. Field kept in the top drawer of his desk. He was quite strict, and had no tolerance for assignments that were not completed, or forgotten at home.

One day Mike had not completed the homework that had been assigned. It was haying season, and there was barely time to get all the chores done at night, let alone find an opportunity to sit down and dream up an English essay.

Mr. Field had no pity for what he considered Mike's misguided priorities.

"You will stay after school until the assignment is completed!" he thundered, as he pointed with a wooden yardstick at Mike's quite-empty notebook page.

Mike was thunderstruck. This was the worst punishment he could have been given. He thought of the chain reaction of problems this created, as he scribbled feverishly. The other kids were waiting outside for him to drive them home with the team. It would be late when they got home, and all the chores awaited them. They would all be mad at him.

His father would also be furious when he saw that the milk cows weren't brought in on time – his mother would have to wait supper for them – it would throw the entire family into an unfamiliar routine.

The faster he scribbled, the longer Mr. Field kept him in, complaining that it wasn't neat enough, and making him redo the messiest section. Finally, he sat down to read Mike's hastily-written essay in what seemed a maddeningly slow fashion.

At long last, he said sternly, "You may go now" – although it had been less than an hour, it seemed like an eternity to Mike.

Grabbing his lunch pail, he tore out to start facing all the other problems.

The rest of the day was a chain reaction of rushing the horses, being late getting the milk cows and doing the chores, and getting yelled at, and being late for supper, as he had expected. It was something he never forgot, and far worse than any threshing with the strap.

Recess and lunch hours were spent playing baseball. There were no recreational supplies for the schools back then – no bats, balls, or a face mask or padded vest for the backcatcher. They used sticks and rocks, or anything else hard they could find to substitute for a ball. Mr. Field wanted the children to each bring ten cents to school, in order to buy a softball and a bat. This proved to be impossible for most of the children.

They did have a sponge-ball to play anti-I-over, and they made a swing from ropes and a board seat hung from a tree; and a teeter-totter was fashioned by balancing a rail over the hitching post.

Summertime found these children at the swimming hole. It was a welcome finale to their work-filled days in the hot weather, despite the mud and the bloodsucking leeches.

When winter blew in and installed a thick layer of ice on the lake, hockey was the highlight. They used the rubber heel from someone's boot for a puck. Old rubber boots were used for skates, those who could manage it added blades to their boots. All manner of things were tied overtop of winter boots to make them slippery. Mike's Dad would go to the willow thicket with his knife, and find willow sticks with just the right crook to fashion hockey sticks. The referee was Edna Stafford. Wire netting attached to boards served as makeshift goals. Home-made skis were fashioned from barrel staves and trees and tied onto their boots.

From the time that Mike Isnardy was old enough to comprehend anything, he didn't want to ever be categorized along with the many children in this family – the house was full of babies and domestic duties – he wanted to be a man right from the start.

He did as he was asked in the house, and took his turn helping out on washday. He hauled water to the round galvanized washtub outside in the yard, with the well-worn old glass scrub board and brush; he hauled clean water in and dirty water out, for the Saturday night bath ritual, and made sure there was a constant supply of dry wood stacked by the stove. On Saturday nights, everyone took their turn in the washtub, now hauled into the kitchen and serving as a bathtub, with a blanket hung up for privacy. The last one to bath was sure to have the dirtiest and the coldest water. He helped to look after the younger children on many occasions.

All of this was time he put in until he could escape to the outdoor world of men and animals – the roughness and toughness of the elements and the work. No-one could ever tell him that he was too little or too weak or too young to do something.

One of Mike's jobs was to feed the pigs, usually ten or twelve. Twice a day, he would build a fire, and balance two forty-five gallon barrels on rocks over the fire, and cook up potatoes and grain together with water. He did this a day ahead of time, so that he always had a batch to feed them that wasn't hot. When the sows were farrowing, he made sure they had proper bedding, and that they were left in peace with nobody bothering them. A root cellar was dug, built in to the ground, about fifty yards long, which was used to store the animals after butchering – pigs, sheep, beef, chickens, turkeys; quarters of meat hung to tenderize and cure before being hauled to the butcher shop in Williams Lake.

Mike now involved himself with the task of helping to get the crucial hay supply in for the winter. The hay was cut and piled into stacks, with a team pulling a sloop built by his father. The cumbersome stacks had to be packed down in order to pile as much as possible on the top.

Mike now got his turn at driving the gang plow that would be driven on top of the stacks to pack down the hay. This involved harnessing up a team of five – three horses and two mules – and coaxing them up over top of the hay stack and down the other side. Harnessing these massive horses took some finagling for a six-year-old boy. Mike would maneuver Frank, the big brown stud, close to the fence. He would then climb onto the fence, lug the harness up, and slide it across the horse's back. To put on the collar, he would position it upside down around the huge neck and buckle it. He would then push it up close to his head to the smaller part of his neck, turn the collar right-side-up and let it slide back to his shoulders. Then he would put the hames on to the collar and buckle it up. The backbands and tugs followed in similar but easier sequence.

As the years went by, harnessing the work horses became a routine and simple task for Mike, as he grew taller and stronger, and became able to throw the heavy harness on with ease and confidence. The buckles and snaps and chains became so familiar that he probably could have harnessed the teams and hooked them to the wagons with his eyes shut.

The mules, Jack and Jenny, were invaluable for packing down the hay, as their hooves were small and sharp, and they were very sure-footed on the sometimes slippery hay slope. They were smaller than the massive draft horses, and wouldn't sink down so far into the stack. Mike loved to harness the mules and drive them up onto the fluffy hay stacks, packing them down to make room for more to be piled on top, and prevent the wind from blowing away all their labours.

Rock-picking was an ongoing duty, as this was a very rocky area. Mike would harness up Jack the Mule to a stoneboat – a flat apparatus that dragged on the ground behind the mule, and rocks could be thrown onto it and transported off the field. It was built from a couple of pieces of small logs five feet long and six inches in diameter, with a couple of sticks nailed across to hold them the right distance apart. Boards were nailed on top, so it could be used to haul almost anything. Once again, the mule's small sharp feet were better-suited for picking his way amongst the rocks, than the heavy-footed larger draft horses.

Alice helped Mike pick rocks. Sometimes they would get over-zealous and pile too many rocks on the stoneboat, making it too heavy for the mule to pull. Jack, being a typical mule, would flatten back his ears, straighten out his front legs and sit back on his haunches, refusing to budge. This called for special consideration, and Mike learned that if he went up to old Jack and whispered in his hairy ear, the mule would get going again. Mike would never tell anyone exactly what it was he said to that mule.

This rig was also used to clean the barn out all winter, manure forked into huge piles outside, to be hauled out on to the fields as precious fertilizer in the spring.

Harness had to be looked after, and this was a massive job every spring. Piles upon piles of harness would be laid out and oiled before the summer work started again. This would keep the leather from cracking and becoming too stiff to handle. The draft horses were monstrous and strong – it was important to keep the harness needed to control them in good repair. No-one wanted a line to break when trying to hold back a pair of feisty young horses.

Harry Roper was a friend of Mike's Dad, and a frequent unannounced cheerful visitor who would show up and sleep on the floor. He always brought moccasins or gloves that his wife had made. Mike took a liking to

Harry and tried his best not to be sent to bed at the usual time when Harry was there. He watched in interest at the numbers of sweaters that this native Indian always wore. His wife spun wool and knitted with it afterwards. When he came in the winter, he would be wearing about six sweaters, the largest one on the outside came down to his knees. They were usually quite crooked, as he would have the buttons in the wrong buttonholes. After sitting in the house for awhile with the warmth of the wood stove, he would start removing sweaters. Within an hour he would be down to his shirtsleeves and there would be a pile of sweaters in the corner.

In 1931 a baby girl Rita was born. Mike was eight years old, and had experienced the births of six babies now in the home where he lived. He had run to fetch his father James to the house at that critical time, and hurriedly followed the orders to heat up some water on the stove, and to get a clean blanket ready for the newborn.

He would watch as James would sterilize a special knife for cutting the umbilical cord, and head to the bedroom to coax and assist Evelyn as she strained and groaned, eventually pushing out another tiny person to be welcomed into the eagerly waiting clan. There was always relief when the infant made its first cry, and excitement in waiting their turn to hold him or her, and have a close personal look at the newest Isnardy creation.

The Isnardy children, and in fact all the children striving to grow up in a time where money and possessions were both hard to come by, were always on the lookout for some way in which to make some kind of income. Alice wrote a business letter on behalf of herself and Mike, applying for the job of janitor at the school. Mr. Charles Harris was the secretary of the local school district, and Alice very carefully and painstakingly wrote a very formal business-like letter.

One day an official-looking letter came to the farm with the weekly mail, addressed to Alice. With great excitement, she tore open the letter – yeah – she was chosen for the job, with pay of three dollars per month. She and Mike took the job on in earnest, making sure the floors were always clean, the blackboards erased, the water and wood supply hauled and the barn kept clean. The school was the center of social activities for the community, and needed to be kept in prime cleanliness.

Every year on Good Friday, the Anglican minister Rev. Resker used to show lantern slides. These were slide shows shown on the wall in the school – the slides had to be moved by hand. Everyone was mesmerized, and no-one ever missed this show, if they could help it.

At the Alkali Lake Ranch, not far down the road, the weekly movies were a little more sophisticated. Films were Saturday-night entertainment, and greatly anticipated by the entire ranching crew and any neighbours or visitors that happened along. They were shown in the hall, using a projector that was run from the battery of a car that was left running outside. The problem was that some unlucky person had to be in the car keeping the vehicle from stalling, so the projector would continue working. One movie night, the film suddenly speeded up and was going faster and faster, clearly out of control.

When the movie-goers ran out to see what was happening, they found the guy who was keeping his foot on the gas was asleep, and had fallen onto the gas pedal, revving the motor to its limit. The extra power produced by the battery sent the projector reel spinning at top speed.

Dances, school picnics, ball games, Christmas concerts, church services (Catholic and Anglican) were all held in the one-room country schoolhouses. The Isnardy children were raised in the comfortable shelter of their farm life, the security of their siblings and many family members, and the neighbours in the surrounding community. They had not been exposed to other people and places; most of them had never been to town.

1932 was a monumental year for Mike. This was his first trip to town – he and Alice were to attend communion ceremony. Father McIntyre of the Roman Catholic diocese, or Father Resker of the Anglican Church, performed these ceremonies; but this particular time Archbishop William Mark Duke was coming from Vancouver to perform the special service. It was an important and special day.

This warranted a haircut for Mike. He was sat down on a stool with a towel secured around his neck, as his father snipped away at his hair. Dark clumps fell away to be caught on the towel, some landed in a growing circle on the board floor. Mike clamped his bare toes around the rung of the stool to ensure he sat as still as possible to avoid any wayward nicks to his ears or, worse yet, a bald spot left by a slip of the swift-snipping blades.

All shirts and trousers in the house were inspected to find the ones that were closest to his fit and not in need of repairs. The suitable outfit was then washed with great care; the heavy flat iron was heated on the stove and used to flatten every crease from the precious shirt and pants. The best pair of dress shoes that were close to Mike's fit were polished until they shone.

Alice was undergoing the same treatment – the best dress in the house that was close to her size was washed, ironed, and hung with great care, not to be worn until the day of the communion, to guard against any accidents. All the girls' shoes in the house were inspected, a growing pile in the middle of the floor, until a pair suitable in size and appropriateness was chosen to be buffed up for the occasion. Her sisters and her mother curled and re-curled her hair, tying strips of rags around the tresses to form curls – putting it up, brushing it down again, agreeing and disagreeing on a suitable hairdo.

The washtub was hauled in to the middle of the kitchen, and filled with pails of steaming water from the stove. After they had scrubbed themselves as clean as possible, Evelyn inspected the results with the scrutinizing eye of a mother, pulling Mike's ears ahead to make sure he had not missed any areas.

Although nine-year-old Mike and eight-year-old Alice were rough and tough and had no fear of bushes and wild animals and all the situations that could happen and did happen in their lives on the farm, heading to town was absolutely alien to them. They were excited, but terrified.

The big day arrived, and they set out on the twenty-mile ride by team and wagon to Williams Lake, wide-eyed to all the new area they passed along the way. Finally they trotted down the long hill of the Dog Creek Road into the town settlement. Mike and Alice were speechless with uncertainty and wonder. This was unfamiliar territory – strange people going about their business amid the streets and storefronts, teams with buggies and wagons, buzzing activity. They followed the explicit directions that had been given them and headed straight for the house of their older sister Dorothy, now married to Roy Haines.

Dorothy welcomed them warmly and made them feel at home. After a bit of a visit, she felt that Mike and Alice would be anxious to see what was inside one of those stores, especially the line-up of glass jars filled with various sticks of colored hard candy. She asked them to run to the Post Office, two blocks away, and mail a letter. She gave them a nickel for the stamp and told them they could buy themselves some candy at the store with the change. Wide-eyed with great excitement, and anticipating their first steps inside a store to purchase candy after their errand was accomplished, they set off eagerly.

They had gone about a block and would now have to turn the corner where they wouldn't be able to see the house anymore. This proved to be too much for them. They got scared, turned around and ran back to Dorothy's home.

They didn't get the letter mailed, and didn't get the candy.

Carl Frizzi cutting James Isnardy's hair

Mules packing hay

Isnardy children beside Church

In 1933, another baby was born – a boy they named Norman. Mike celebrated his tenth birthday, and decided it was time he had a business of his own. He had already tried a few enterprises: selling seed packets for McFayden Seeds, for 30% profit; selling Christmas cards – six for a nickel – he tired of both these undertakings very quickly.

His cousin Bill Isnardy gave him a wild yearling colt, although it was quite crippled. Wondering what to do with this lame horse, as it was of no use, he traded it to their neighbour Pete Tresierra, who was looking for something to use as coyote bait. The trade was supposed to be for two turkey hens.

Mike harnessed up Jiggs and Steve to the sleigh, and headed off to Pete's place to close the deal – to deliver the colt and pick up the turkeys. It was about eight miles to Pete's farm, which proved to be quite a trip for the skinny malnourished young horse. His crippled leg had prevented him from keeping up with the rest of the wild herd when he needed nourishment.

When he finally arrived at Pete's place, Pete walked around and around the colt; finally, scratching his chin, he shook his head – " this horse ain't worth two turkeys – I'll give you one for 'im".

Mike was in no mood to argue the merits of this sad little cayuse. He accepted the gnarly feet of the black turkey hen that Pete held out to him, stuffed it into a gunny sack he had brought along just for that purpose, and tied it onto the sleigh with a rope. He cast one last look at the forlorn wild little colt and whispered aloud as he untied the reins and climbed back onto the sleigh, "you might not be the finest horse around, but you're a damn sight prettier'n this turkey!"

The turkey hen survived the winter and, when spring came around, Mike started pondering how he could find a turkey gobbler for his hen so that he could get into production of more turkeys. It just so happened that his aunt Ethel Stafford was raising turkeys, and had a few gobblers. She allowed Mike to bring his lady turkey over to spend time with her turkey gobbler for breeding purposes. He left her there for two weeks.

After he brought the hen home again, she started laying eggs. Now he had to persuade his mother to allow him to stick the turkey eggs underneath some chickens that were setting on eggs of their own. She agreed, and in a month or so, Mike excitedly watched fluffy turkey chicks hatch out of the eggs.

It wasn't long before he was seeing them change from cute little fluff-balls when they hatched out, to big warted replicas of their parents. That was alright, as Mike figured the uglier they became, the easier it would be to butcher them. Eagerly, he awaited the time when he could cash in on the growing gobblers, and realize some profit from all this high-stake bartering.

By fall, Mike had eighteen turkeys to butcher.

Now although Mike had slaughtered many animals before, from sheep to pigs to chickens, and even cows, he had never butchered a turkey. He managed to get lots of advice from everyone but, strangely, no-one offered to actually help with this job.

"Just hang 'im up by the feet on a hook, and stick 'im through the upper part of the mouth, and all the feathers'll fall right off," he was told. So he grabbed a turkey and hung it up by the feet, and bravely stabbed the knife in where he had been told. The feathers didn't fall out as they were supposed to.

He waited – perhaps it took time. Every once in awhile he would give a good tug on them, but there was nothing loose about those feathers. Finally, he started pulling them out, one feather at a time. This was slow and laborious work, and downright aggravating. As he tugged and pulled away at each feather, he realized it was going to take him a half a day to do one turkey alone. Eighteen turkeys was going to take well over a week, and he had many other chores to do. Frustrated, he began jerking faster and harder at the feathers. He managed to get half the feathers off in this fashion.

Suddenly, he had the strange feeling that he was not

Turkey Business

alone and, looking down, he was horrified to see that the turkey had miraculously come back to life. Cocking its head up from its upside-down position, it looked him straight in the eye, as if to ask just what the heck he thought he was doing.

Mike leaped away from the turkey and, after regaining his composure, searched for his knife to repeat the procedure of sticking the turkey again. This time the turkey was certainly dead, but the feathers did not come out any easier.

Mike mulled over his dilemma for a few days, finding himself, as much as he thought he disliked turkeys, absolutely unable to end their paltry lives in what seemed such a heinous manner. Alternate ways of doing them in would not work, as this was the only process by which the birds would "bleed" properly, so as not to ruin the meat. They had to be killed – winter was coming on, and he would have to buy feed soon to get them through the winter. Already they had gobbled up all the grain and corn mixture he had managed to hoard for them.

Finally, one morning, Mike had had enough stress trying to deal with this problem. He hitched up the team and sleigh, stuffed all the turkeys into gunny sacks, and hauled them all the way to Williams Lake to the meat shop to be butchered and sold. This cost him any profits he would have made.

This mattered not to him now – he was SO glad to be rid of the turkeys – even if he didn't make any money, he wouldn't have to look at their forlorn warted faces staring at him when they were half-plucked.

As entertaining as the turkeys were, the Isnardy children had another diversion, now that snow covered the ground – a rambunctious white ram with a black face. He was coal-black and cunning, and the enterprising kids finally found a use for him.

They would lead the reluctant ram quite a ways from the sheep barn – he didn't want to go, it was cold, and the barn was warm. They strained on the rope to haul the ram as far away from the barn as they could. It took two or three of them, digging in their heels one behind the other, to pull the balking ram where they wanted him to go. One strong person had to then hold him securely by the head, while someone else see-sawed the rope back and forth in his thick wool, until it was buried quite securely. At the end of the rope they tied their wooden sleigh, all the time making sure he didn't escape. Then one person would hold the ram so he couldn't run back to the barn, while the others climbed onto the sleigh. This all had to be accomplished as quickly as possible, as the resisting animal fought continuously to escape.

When they were settled on the sleigh, they would yell "Let 'im go!" and the one who was holding the ram would let go of the ram's head, then try his best to leap on to the sleigh with the others as it went flying past him. The ram would head with all his worth back to the barn, and everyone on the sleigh got a great ride, hanging on to each other for dear life, laughing and hollering all the way. They continued this entertainment until they got caught, and had to quit.

This was amusing for the children, but the ram didn't find it at all fun. In fact, he grew to look for opportunities to retaliate against these little monsters. He watched for his chances – any time he could sneak up to within six to eight feet from anybody, he would suddenly lower his head and jump through the air, hitting them right in the rear end, knocking them to the ground. By the time the target of his sneak attack would jump to their feet, he would be standing there smugly.

One day he picked the wrong target. Mike's mother, Evelyn, was peacefully hanging clothes on the clothesline. Enjoying the bright breezy sunshine, she was humming away, a cluster of clothes pins in her mouth.

Suddenly and without warning, she was hit from behind with a force that sent her flying. She soared through the air, landing in a heap in the dirt, enshrouded in previously-clean sheets, diapers and towels, the clothespins flung in every direction.

Infuriated, she looked up and saw the ram standing there thinking he had really accomplished something.

Raging against the tangle of now-dirty laundry around her, she was up and on her feet and, before he knew

*Turkey Business*

what hit him, she grabbed him by the horns. Digging in her heels like a buckle-winning bulldogger, she twisted with all her might,and wrestled him to the ground. Kicking and punching and calling him names that shocked her children, she didn't let go her deathly grip until her fury was spent.

From that time on, it was safer to be around the yard. The ram had learned his lesson, and his manners were noticeably improved.

In summer, the sheep were turned out to range back in the mountains behind the farm. They would stay there, grazing for feed in the abundant meadows and underbrush. When one was needed for butchering, the kids were sent out with the horses to round them up. After one was selected for butchering, the rest were returned to their mountain grazing area. It was the children's responsibility to check on the flock constantly, to ensure that no predators – coyotes, bears, or cougars, were depleting their numbers.

In 1935, another baby girl, Olive, was born and introduced into the busy Isnardy household. Shortly afterwards, in 1936, Mike's half-sister Tillie, who had married Ralph Inscho, gave birth to a baby boy.

Ralph was ecstatic as, after four baby girls, this was finally a son for him. He showed up at the Isnardy house with a packsack filled with a gift for them. Mike and his siblings were overjoyed to see two fluffy puppies, yellow and playful little border collies. Mike could hardly wait for them to get a little bigger, so he could start training them to mind the sheep and cattle herds.

James Isnardy harnessed up the team to the buggy, and everyone piled in to visit the new addition. Baby Ray Inscho was born at the foot of Pablo Mountain, at what was known as the Petrowitz Place.

1936 also saw the birth of another baby boy into the Isnardy clan. Fred was born, and the family adjusted itself once again, wiggling around to make room for yet another. Each new baby was greeted with happiness and joy. There were many willing arms standing in line for their turn to hold and snuggle a newcomer, and make him feel welcome and loved.

Mike Isnardy itching to head out on a cattle drive

Mike and sisters Alice and Ollie, 1937

# The Ghost of Boitano Place

Later that fall of 1936, when everyone was preoccupied with the many tasks that accompanied threshing, a tragedy struck the neighbourhood, leaving fear and apprehension in its wake. A neighbour by the name of Lawrence Roberts, living close to the Springhouse School, shot his wife and then himself.

The event sent shock waves around the district. Buggies and wagons came and went, neighbours reaching out to each other with tidbits of information; the adults talking in hushed tones, resorting to sudden silence when any children came into the room. Grim looks, hurried movements, everyone with their own quiet opinions about why this happened – "should have seen the signs" – "should have done something" – children were afraid to head to the outhouse after dark; protective fathers stayed close to home, pulling their families in close around them, like comfortable old coats.

Johnny Hutch was one of the neighbours, living now in a cabin he owned at George Moore's Spokin Lake Ranch on the road to Horsefly. He had moved there from the Lawrence Boitano place. One of his favorite pastimes was telling ghost stories.

One late fall day following the Roberts tragedy, he was back visiting with the Isnardy family. Darkness fell early, and Johnny, true to form, delivered a dramatic story about how he tried to leave the Spokin Lake Ranch one day. He had saddled up his horse, and proceeded at a trot up the road, anxious to get to his destination. At a certain spot by a dark grove of trees that moved ominously in the wind, the horse snorted, sidestepped, and danced around, refusing to go any further. Finally, when coaxing and force failed to work, Johnny was left with no choice but to turn the unyielding horse around and head back towards the barn. Everything seemed to be fine now, so he decided to try once more. Back he got to the same spot on the road, and the horse again refused to travel past this point.

Johnny claimed it was a ghost that stopped him from proceeding on his way. He finally rode back to the barn, put his horse away, and stayed for the night.

Mike was now a teenager, thirteen years old, and was very much affected by Johnny Hutch's ghostly accounts, and all the other frightening stories that the tragedy had left circulating around the neighbourhood. After listening wide-eyed to one of the stories, he was scared to go out in the dark. When his Mom called to him, "Mike, can you please bring potatoes up from the cellar?", his heart sank to the soles of his feet – to get to the cellar, he had to go outside – in the *dark*. He stalled and stalled, until finally his Mom said in a threatening tone *"MIKE"* – and he knew he couldn't put it off any longer. He remembered what had happened to the ram, and decided even facing a ghost was preferable to what would happen to him if he didn't fetch those potatoes.

Picking up a coal oil lantern to light his way, he opened the door, gingerly looked in both directions around the corner, then raced as fast as he could to the cellar.

Once inside, he gathered up the potatoes, trying to ignore the ghostly shadows that danced in front and behind him from the lantern bobbing in his hand. Then, struggling with potatoes in one hand and the lantern in the other, he hesitated at the door as he took a deep breath and again pelted, as fast as he could, back to the safety of the house.

Slamming the door behind him, he practically threw the pail of potatoes at his mother.

"What's wrong with you, Mike, you look like you've seen a ghost!?" she chided him.

The next morning, Mike's Dad was waiting when he woke up. Mike's insides churned when he saw the angry look on his father's face.

Mike had been in such a hurry to get back to the house before the ghost caught him that he had not shut the cellar door properly. "You were the last one in the cellar last night, and the door wasn't shut tight! You're lucky it didn't get cold enough to freeze everything in there, or we'd all starve to death this winter!", yelled his father.

The precious winter supply of vegetables for the entire family was at risk of being ruined, and he was not allowed to forget that for awhile.

Mike's two half-sisters, Dorothy and Irene, and two of the Hutch girls, used to walk up to the Lawrence Boitano place, now owned by Johnny and Nellie Hutch. They, too, were afraid of the darkness.

One dark night under a cold distant moon that made eerie shadows in the night, the four girls ran to the barn to ready some horses, as they were too frightened to be on foot. The four of them headed out in the moonlight for the Hutch home. Hurrying the horses through the dark bushes, they were relieved to reach the main road without incident, where the openness and the moonlight seemed a safer place to be. They relaxed a bit, talking and giggling.

There were many local stories that when told and retold in the darkness, were enough to terrify even the stout-hearted. One of their favorites was of the two Frenchmen who were murdered just a few miles from where they now rode. Two travelling adventurers had come all the way from the California goldfields on foot, and Grandpa Amedee Isnardy had hired them to build a store for him. They had their worldly goods with them, which included gold, money and a number of gold watches. When they didn't show up for work, a search was conducted. One body was found floating in the lake, the other would not be found until years later when a young lady was swimming in the lake and stepped on the skull.

The murderers were caught and hanged for this crime, but the valuables the victims had carried with them were never found. A local native offered the information that the loot was buried under a big tree in the area known today as the Springhouse Trails Ranch. Although the following generations of the area families dug many holes under many big trees, the valuables were never unearthed.

Then there were the five Indian maidens who hanged themselves further south down the Dog Creek Road on which the frightened girls were now trotting. Five graves, side by side and sunken on the side mountain above Dog Creek, still mark this event today, under the same tree where they were all found hanging one morning.

Dog Creek was named after an old chief Skaha, meaning "dog" in the local Shuswap dialect. Chief Skaha was noted for his prowess as a warrior. The five young Indian women apparently all found themselves the objects of the insincere affections of a "white bounder". When they discovered he was playing fast and loose with their affections, they rode up the mountain with ropes and were all found hanging there the following morning.

All these events seemed frighteningly close, as the two Isnardy girls and the two Hutch girls now trotted along in the eerie darkness along the main road above the Springhouse Trails ranch house.

Suddenly and unbelievably, a white apparition appeared on the road ahead. It seemed to come out of nowhere, and stood quite still now in the middle of the road, as if waiting for them to come further. The terrified girls, paralyzed in fear, fought to control the prancing horses. As they pulled senselessly on the reins, the horses went around and round in a snorting turmoil, unsure what their agitated and befuddled riders wanted. As they watched, transfixed, the shrouded figure raised its arms in the air, and began gliding towards them.

Amidst screeches and screams, and heels desperately digging in and kicking the horses in their ribs, they spun around and galloped all the way back to the yard. Not bothering to take time for the barn, they abandoned their horses in front of the house, and rushed inside, falling over each other, and slamming the door closed behind them. Babbling and scared to death, they rushed to peer out the window to see if the specter had followed them.

All they saw was their father, James, walking nonchalantly back towards the house, a white sheet tucked discreetly under his jacket.

Calmly, he gathered up the fallen reins from the milling horses, and led them to the barn.

Ghosts and spirits weren't restricted to the

Springhouse area. Without the benefit of television and computers with their endless bombardment of entertainment, people resorted to the stories and tales as a diversion from their toil-filled lives.

Big Francis Kazam was a Chilcotin Indian well-known in the local Blackwater area for his witch-doctor powers. One day he was approached by another Indian who asked for his help in ridding his wife of an evil spirit that he believed had invaded her. Big Francis complied, and followed the man to his cabin, where his wife was stretched out on a cot.

Big Francis donned a special costume of skins and feathers, and waving some branches around while chanting and mumbling, he danced around and around the still form of the unfortunate Indian woman. Suddenly, he made a grab at the air with both hands and shouted, "I have it! I caught the evil spirit!! What shall I do with it now??"

The Indian girl's husband noted that his wife was still quite lifeless, and not believing anymore in Big Francis' powers, yelled "Shove it!".

Big Francis ended up at the home of a man by the name of Ed Adams, who also had his doubts about Big Francis and his spirit powers. Following a large supper of beef stew, Big Francis complained of a stomach ache and retired to bed, where he suffered with abdominal spasms throughout the night.

The following morning, Ed Adams asked Big Francis if he had slept well. Big Francis replied that he had spent the night fighting with the devil.

Ed Adams was quick to respond that he, too, had heard a commotion in the night, in particular a ghostly voice that had spoken very clearly the words – "I'll get him on the mountain."

This information caused Big Francis to become quite weak in the knees. Although it was his habit to camp overnight on the mountain on his way home, from that day onward he made the trip home in one day.

He never camped on the mountain again.

Father McIntyre and
James Isnardy

Amadee and Richard

Norman and Frank

# The Working Man

## Chapter 6

It was 1937 and Mike Isnardy was growing up. Tall and muscled and strong, he now classified himself as a man, at the age of fourteen. He wanted to do more than the daily chores at home – he craved men's work. He felt much more designed to work with the heavy horse teams and whatever equipment, like threshers or hay sloops or ploughs, than to be confined to the garden with a hoe or, worse yet, delegated to churn butter or babysit.

One day he and Ken were sent out to weed three rows of potatoes. This doesn't sound like a lot, but each row was over a quarter of a mile in length. It didn't take long before the barefoot boys tired of this monotonous job and began to search out a more entertaining pastime. They got down into the dirt and built "corrals" out of the soil. Then they caught ladybugs. Ladybugs were everywhere – friendly pretty spotted orange bugs that are actually welcomed in a garden, as they feed on aphids that are mainly on the underside of the leaves. Their corral was filled with ladybugs, and not much work was getting done when their mother showed up to find out why the weeding was taking so long. They had to go back to hoeing and, to add insult to injury, the ladybugs all flew away.

Their Dad decided to send them to a different job – the grass had grown up under the electric fence that kept the milk cows from wandering. They kept moving this electric fenced "corral" around so that the cows would have fresh pasture. Mike and Ken were sent to pull all the grass from under the fence. They finished quickly, all the while daring each other to touch the electric fence to see if it was working. Neither one would touch it. Finally Ken decided to pee on it, just to see what would happen. His body flew straight up in the air, then fell over backwards. Mike rolled on the ground with laughter, this diversion had definitely been worth the entertainment.

Mike began to work in the summer for a Dane by the name of Ingvard Johnson, whose farm was at Springhouse. Ingvard Johnson was an elderly bachelor, who really liked his horses. He also had a faithful old sorrel dog called Neaho, which meant 'lightning' in Danish. Neaho was eighteen years old and somehow always managed to ride, and not to walk. When the teams were working, he would ride on the buggy or the sleigh. He would jump to the saddle on the saddle horse and ride along – Ingvard had a horse called Throl, a heavy bay horse, which meant 'thunder' in Danish.

Ploughing was done with a four-horse percheron team, and Mike was given this job one year. The horses were well cared for, constantly grain-fed. Usually there were some fields that didn't get ploughed in the fall, and had to be done the following spring. This year Mike ploughed until December 24th and got them all done, which impressed Ingvard a great deal. There were rustle fences to be fixed, and downed timber in the fields that needed to be piled and burned.

Ingvard grew a lot of grain – he needed a good amount of grain to feed to his teams of massive work horses. Porcupines and woodchucks (yellow marmots) loved the grain fields, and Ingvard was constantly trying to keep them away from his precious grain, and supplied Mike with a twelve gauge shotgun and shells. Mike shot a lot of porcupines, and countless woodchucks – he could sometimes shoot three woodchucks with one shot, as they piled up together around the rock piles where they had their dens.

At Ingvard's, there was always a "green" horse that needed to be trained, and Mike broke his first work horse, a young percheron. Ingvard had the occasional runaway with his teams.

Ingvard Johnson had to pack water quite a ways to his place, probably a quarter of a mile. He fashioned a strong stick which he carried across his shoulders. About a foot or two of rope hung down from each end of the stick, with hooks to carry water pails.

Ingvard was a hardworking pioneer, and a very nice man to work for, but unfortunately had some medical problems. There seemed to always be something wrong with his head, and finally he went to Kamloops for an operation, and died there. He had sold his farm to Oliver Hardy. Today Eric Stafford owns this piece of property.

It was pretty confusing in the district, as there were two men by the name of Sam Sorenson. Almost unbelievably they lived within a few miles of each other, and were not even remotely related, even though their names were spelled exactly the same. One had come from Washington and the other from Montana. To avoid confusion, they were referred to as "Washington Sam" and "Montana Sam".

Montana Sam and Ingvard were business partners, in that they shared a threshing machine. This huge machine, as well as the unit that powered it, were moved with teams back and forth between the two places. Billy Pinchbeck also had a threshing machine that made its way around the district.

Mike went to work for Montana Sam, who was a meticulous fussy farmer – everything had to be just so. Mike was hired to plant the garden, and the first row he planted was not absolutely straight. Sam planted the rest of the rows, and they grew up in straight orderly fashion. He joked about Mike's crooked row, remarking that "even the crooked row grew" and then pointing out that there would be more vegetables in the crooked row than in the straight ones. Even his grain fields had to be in line – any weeds growing in the grain had to be pulled out, packed into a gunnysack and hauled off the field to be burned. Dandelion roots had to be dug, hauled off and burned as well.

One rainy day Sam Sorenson took the opportunity to head to Williams Lake to do business, and left Mike to pick rocks off the field with the team and wagon. Mike kept picking rocks in the rain, anxious to get the job done. When Sam returned from town, he ran out to stop Mike from working, as he claimed the dirt was sticking to the wheels, and the topsoil was being carried off the field on the wagon wheels.

Montana Sam Sorenson sold his place to Reidemans; it ended up belonging to Herricks.

Washington Sam died, but before he did, he sold his place to Lloyd Stafford.

Mike started doing what he loved best – herding cattle. The further the move, the happier he was. To be able to pack up a saddlebag, tie a bedroll on behind, and head out through the forests to the meadows where the cattle needed to be taken to fresh grass – that was where he wanted to be.

Frank Armes was running the Dog Creek Ranch for a Colonel Spencer, who also owned the Pavilion Ranch. The steers had to be moved from one operation to the other, and the cows with their new calves needed to be brought back. An elderly gentleman from Alkali, originally from Dog Creek, Moffatt Jack, was the cook in the chuckwagon. He presided over a huge blackened pot that hung over the fire, simmering with some concoction of stew, with lots of beans and potatoes. Mike looked forward to finding out what was in the huge pot each night, as they settled the herd of three hundred and fifty cows down, looked after their horses, then headed for the cook's wagon for a plate. They were always famished.

These were wet years. When the cattle drive was completed, the hay situation needed attention. With the monsoon-like weather, there was a problem with keeping the haystacks from getting too soaked, and heating up on the inside. It was necessary to dump salt into the inside of the stacks in some way, to keep them from burning up.

"Hurry up with that salt!!" yelled Pete Rasmussen, as he balanced himself on top of a stack that was already burning, smoke pluming out the top. He hurriedly dug down from the top, the smoke becoming thicker as he opened up air space down to the smouldering hay. Quickly he placed a half dozen logs inside, to be a base for the one hundred pound sacks of salt to be dumped inside. He stood on the top, while fourteen-year-old Mike and anyone else they could commandeer hoisted the hundred pound sacks onto their shoulders and laboured up the slippery hay stack to him. Eventually the smoke stopped spiralling out from the salty-smelling hay "chimney" and they could relax for awhile. They hauled a few more sacks to be dumped in, just for good measure. Later the cows would all walk around with brown noses, from eating the salt-soaked hay.

Now Mike was offered his first real steady job off the farm, for Ted Weetman at Brunson Lake.

The offer was $1 a day, and Mike worked there off and on for three years. When the time came to settle up, Ted Weetman called Mike into the farmhouse, and handed him an envelope full of bills.

"I know I hired you on at $1 a day, Mike, because you were so young, but I am now paying you $1.50 a day. You did just as much work as the older men, so you should be paid the same," he claimed as he clapped Mike across the back. This was music to Mike's sixteen-year-old ears.

He had raked all of the hay, and had run the hay sloop to stack it afterwards. In wet weather, he didn't sit idle – there was wood to be cut with a cross-cut saw. There was also another cattle drive to Williams Lake. There was never a time when there was not work to be done. Having someone reward him justly for his hard work spurred him on.

The following summer haying was interrupted with rainy weather. The rain seemed to go on forever, with half the meadows already stacked. The other half of the meadow ended up under about a foot, and in some places, two feet of water.

Ted Weetman was becoming very concerned about the seemingly endless deluge from the sky, and what it was doing to his all-important hay crop. He told Mike to go home for awhile, thinking it would stop raining and the meadow would hopefully dry up again. Putting up wet hay was not a good plan.

It never did get dry, and in a cold wet and miserable November he called Mike to come back and help stack hay in the water, there was nothing else that could be done. The hay was crucial for winter feed, no matter what shape it was in.

In the morning everything was covered with a brittle layer of ice. They tried standing on the stack, slipping, and getting soaking wet from forking the sodden heavy hay.

Ted Weetman was on one hay sloop, and Mike on the other. A man by the name of Stonewall Jackson was stacking. Stonewall Jackson was an elderly prospector who spent his summers on foot with a blanket and goldpan and a pack on his back. He was happy to find some work to wile away the long winter hours until he could be off on his search for nuggets after the spring thaws. But this job was testing his stamina. Forkful after cumbersome forkful, they managed to fill slings with the sodden hay; when they pulled the sling up in the air, the water would pour out like a waterfall. They put up three stacks in that fashion, a wet burdensome and exhausting job, afterwards they had to dump bags and bags of the heavy salt in these stacks, all the time struggling to stand upright on the icy slippery mounds. The added expense of the tons of salt that was required, and the worsening condition of the feed hay was downright discouraging.

When the wet season turned to winter, Mike was back to feed this same hay to the cattle. By this time, the stacks had frozen to solid ice, and axes had to be used to cut some of the hay. Then they were forced to use crowbars and poles to pry the hay apart in the stacks, all the while fighting to keep from falling off the glacier-like stacks. But it was feed, and essential to keep the cattle alive – it was better than no feed at all. It was a desperate situation.

Winter was just as busy as summer. Two hundred and ten head of cattle needed to be fed every day. It took twice as long to feed these animals with the hay in its frozen condition. It had to be chopped, forked onto the feed wagon, then forked off again to the hungry animals, who chomped hungrily at the icy chunks. It was a tiring and draining procedure, and Mike felt sorry for the animals, who had to work extra hard to get any nutrition from the solid wet feed.

The cattle also needed to be watered every day. This required a watering hole to be cut through the ice on the lake. They would chop with the axe a long hole that was only kept open at one end. This ensured that, if a cow slipped, there wasn't room for them to fall through. This hole was continually freezing over, and had to be constantly checked and kept open. Ice chunks were scooped out of the open drinking hole to make it easier for the cows.

Rails for building fences were cut in the winter. Mike used to cut about one hundred and fifty to two hundred rails after feeding the cattle, all with the axe. The axe had to be constantly sharpened with a file, as a dull axe was asking for disaster. He would cut trees down and chop them into fifteen foot lengths and split them, getting four rails out of one length on the bigger ones, and two out of the smaller ones. Twisted trees were difficult to split, as the grain didn't run straight. One tree would produce about three lengths. The top of the tree would be stripped on two sides, as it was not big enough for splitting.

There was firewood to be cut with a cross-cut saw. One spring they had to cut house logs out of fir trees, and peel them. Andrew Mouse, a native from Sugar Cane, was a carpenter who did fine work with logs, but he needed lumber to work with. After peeling the logs, Mike would flatten one side of the cut logs. The only way was to hue them with a broad axe. His first attempts were slow and uneven, but with practice he became faster and a smoother finish was accomplished. These were then used to make a kitchen, and to add on to an existing house.

In 1941, Mike was eighteen and went to work for his Aunt Matilda at the Pinchbeck Ranch. One hundred and fifty head of cattle needed to be fed, and of course, enough hay put up to accomplish this. Logs needed to be cut to build a log fence. At haying time he worked with Leonard Carolan, Charlie Westwick, and Ken Isnardy. They built "worm fence" which were log fence panels that crisscrossed and notched together, peeled on two sides.

In the fall, he left to work for Fred Stafford, ploughing with a six-horse team. Later Fred became quite sick. His brother and sister, Lloyd and Ethel, took him to Ashcroft Hospital as the Williams Lake Hospital was closed down during the war time. He was later moved to Vancouver for treatment of a seemingly unknown illness. He passed away there nearly a year later.

At the time of Fred's death, Mike was camped out by

himself. He was away from his camp one day checking for broken fences and lost cows; he returned to find a note in his tent that Fred had died.

That night, a great and heavy sadness pervaded him as he sat alone by his campfire.

Ron & Norman

Amadee, Norman, Richard, Fred    Isnardy photo
Springhouse

B runson Lake one winter was totally frozen over, a beautiful clear ice with not a fragment of snow on it. The right combination of winter wind and frigid temperatures had left it mirrorlike and shiny; it beckoned invitingly to Mike and Wilfred Weetman as they jounced over frozen lumps on the feed sleigh. When the feeding was done, they couldn't resist grabbing their worn old skates and heading on to the ice. At one end of the lake was a dam, surrounded by a little open water. It didn't look dangerous.

This was a welcome break from the tedium of hard work they were used to. They were in their late teens, and tried to imitate the famous hockey players they were starting to hear about. For awhile they swooped around and around in large circles, long strong strides slicing up the glassy transparency of the lake's surface. They soon tired of this.

They began a daredevil game – to see who could skate closest to the open water by the dam. Mike whizzed by first, next Wilfred, who glided in a little bit closer than Mike had, leaving his skate track confidently as a marker in the ice.

Then Mike had to go a little closer than Wilfred had. He swung in and raked his skate blade triumphantly further in than Wilfred's last mark.

Wilfred was next, and he travelled right along the edge with two skates on the ice. Mike watched this last act thoughtfully – to better that, he was going to have to be pretty daring. He decided to skate right next to the hole, holding one leg up over the open water. Wilfred would have to do some fancy footwork to outdo this performance.

Boldly, he pointed his skates and pushed off on his blades. As he neared the edge, he lifted one leg as high in the air over the open water as he could muster, with a ballerina-like flourish, his other foot following the edge of the ice.

Before he knew what had happened, he was under the icy cold water. In shock, he wondered where he was and, realizing he was under the water, wondered why he felt no cold, only a sudden adrenalin-packed panic to find the hole through which he had fallen.

Forcing himself to stop flailing, he let the churning water and debris settle around him until he could look up and see the lighted icy chunks which marked his only exit from this watery graveyard. Propelling himself upwards, his lungs ready to burst, he broke through the opening like a trick dolphin. Gasping for air, he found Wilfred desperately crawling around the hole trying to find him. A few minutes later, with Wilfred's help, he lay wet and frozen on top of the ice.

Now the reality of the situation hit him – the freezing temperature, and him with his sopping wet body and clothing. His hair was already frozen solid. He had nothing but his soaking wet skates for his feet, and the laces were already frozen solid – in the time it would take for their numbed fingers to get the skates off, he would probably freeze to death.

They quickly decided it was useless and time-consuming to take all the wet clothes off. The Weetman house was the closest place for help, and they had to skate the full length of the lake. The faster they could get there, the better.

It was the wildest skate they had ever done – a race against the elements – to get Mike to a place of warmth to be able to shed his frozen cocoon. Mike knew that he must keep moving to avoid hypothermia, he was already shivering uncontrollably from the wind created by his fast flight.

Finally they reached the end of the lake, and Mike now had to remove the frozen skates so he could navigate the further distance to the house. Wilfred's fingers were not as frozen as Mike's and he managed to untie and pull off the now solid icy skates. Mike immediately leapt to his wet socked feet and headed at a clumsy run for the warmth he knew was waiting in the Weetman house.

Ted Weetman was not impressed with their foolhardiness, when they struggled in, and Mike was

An Icy Swim

able to gratefully discard his frozen-solid clothes. They were reminded many times of their good luck, and their inherent stupidity in pitting their wits against the superiority of Mother Nature.

In summer, the lake held its magnetism. Wilfred Weetman was crazy for fishing, and Mike joined him at every opportunity. Mike and his brother Ken were building a rustle fence all the way to George Gill's place – a quarter of a mile fence that made them $125.00 in wages. After haying and building fence all day, they climbed in the old wooden boat, grabbed the oars and went fishing. They carried on in this fashion until they became absolutely sick of eating trout.

Sleigh ride, Long Lake

Isnardy photo

An Icy Swim

Dorothy and Curly Isnardy getting ready to go                    Isnardy photo

Linda Isnardy at Springhouse

Mike was now a full-fledged man of twenty, and had proved his prowess in all areas of work that needed to be performed. His responsible attitude made him much sought-after on the nearby farming and ranching spreads. He was strong and sensible, and as capable as the older men when it came to handling the potentially damaging and dangerous situations that sometimes occurred while managing the heavy draft horses. He took on all kinds of jobs in the neighbourhood for the surrounding outfits, his preference being any job that entailed working with teams.

Runaways were not only a dangerous situation for the drivers of these huge powerful horse teams, but many times resulted in damage being done to machinery, equipment, and valuable harness and bridles. There were many runaways, and still some in the hayfields, after they thought the horses were settled down. Sometimes it didn't take much to spook a team – a sudden change in direction, getting their feet tangled up in the traces, birds flying up, sudden noises, horseflies or bees, young horses still learning the ropes. Good horses and good men died sometimes as the result of a runaway. It was not an occupation for the timid or faint of heart.

Charlie was the team horse that seemed to be responsible for the runaways. There were invariably a few mishaps, but this particular horse had an uncanny link to a suspicious number of runaway situations.

Mike was raking hay one brisk, sunny, but damp spring morning. A thousand pound team of percherons, Charlie and Prince, were hitched to the hay rake. Mike always wanted to get a head start on the workday, and the meadow was still wet from an overnight sprinkling of rain, coupled with dew clinging to the early morning grasses. The hay rake was supposed to travel along the surface of the soil, picking up the straight lines of hay.

On this morning the ground was soft and the rake dug into the dirt, got hung up, and then let go with a jerk. Both horses balked and reared, and Charlie landed with one foot over the tongue that separated him from Prince.

"Whoaa – over, Charlie, Whoaa – " Mike, from his seat behind the team on the hay rake, tried desperately to maneuver Charlie back over the tongue with the lines and, realizing this was not going to work, attempted to settle them so that he could get off and unhook the tongue. This would allow Charlie to get back on his own side.

Before he was able to tie the lines so that he could accomplish this, the horses had resorted to chaos. They took off as though jet-propelled, their feet and legs on top of each other, amid a jumble of lines and traces, oblivious to Mike hauling back on the lines and yelling "Whoa –oa" with all his might.

The bouncing hay rake behind spurred them on and Mike, unable to hang on any longer, flew off the back of the rake like a discarded banana peel. Picking himself up from the ground, he could only watch helplessly as the renegade team with the rake flapping behind, continued their blind frenzied flight.

They ran pell-mell until they crashed into the bush on the side of the field, got caught up in the trees, and could no longer move. They resorted to frothing and stomping around in one spot until Mike got to them and started the dangerous and complicated task of trying to quiet them down from their frenzied condition and untangle them at the same time. It took time to calm them down – talking continuously in a soothing tone, yet keeping firm hold so they would not bolt again.

Then it was necessary to make repairs to the harness and equipment that had been damaged in the wild skirmish.

Charlie was on the hay slip when Ted had a runaway; and again when Ted had a second runaway. Then there was another runaway with the hay sloop. Again it was Charlie and Prince.

Ted Weetman was fixing trips on the slings, and his kids were holding the team. The jingling noise of the chains set them off. As the horses lurched ahead in earnest, the frightened youngsters jumped out of the way.

Ted was left on the sloop, on his hands and knees, unable to stop them or even to stand up. The runaways were fleeing at full speed. Ted, bouncing around on the hay sloop, somehow managed to avoid being thrown off.

Ted hung on until he saw that they were going to slam into a stand of willow trees. Not wanting to be in the middle of the inevitable wreck he saw looming ahead, he rolled off before the horses hit the willows. He landed hard,bouncing on the ground. These runaways always made for precious work hours lost as the damage was repaired, or injuries attended to. Being part of a runaway team was a frightening experience and usually led to much hollering and cursing.

It was decided that Charlie needed some serious attention. Many times the driver of the team would loop the reins over the front of the wagon and move further back on the load to throw bales off, etc., trusting the team to move ahead when told, not needing to be encouraged by the reins. It was a bad situation to have a team horse that could not be trusted.

Ted took over the team of Charlie and Prince. He gave Mike a different team of percherons to work with – larger, but more gentled. They were Bell and Tony, and weighed about fifteen hundred pounds. The decision was made to split up the team of Charlie and Prince, and pair each of them up with one of the gentler team.

Ted remarked that different Indians had tried to break Charlie, and could not get anywhere with him. Mike enjoyed a good challenge, and decided to take on the task of "breaking" Charlie on the side, after he had done his day's work. Little by little, he attempted to gain the horse's trust, and finally was successful in saddling him up and staying on him for awhile.

One Monday morning, he decided to use Charlie as a riding horse to round up a bunch of horses and herd them back to the main yard. He put a saddle on Charlie and rode him down near the Pinchbeck line fence where the other horses were, and started them for home. One of the horses he was herding decided he didn't like the border collie trotting along behind, and took a run at the unsuspecting dog. The dog, in a desperate attempt to avoid that horse, ran right into Charlie's legs. Charlie cut loose from the job at hand, bucking as hard as he could, and Mike went sailing from his saddle, and landed unceremoniously on his backside on the ground. In a flash, he was back on his feet, just in time to watch Charlie take off across the field, saddle and bridle and all, reins flying uselessly in the air.

There was nothing else for Mike to do but walk back to Weetman's and find another saddle horse. A cowboy walking home without his horse was not a pretty sight in Mike's mind, and every step he took made him more determined to get back on Charlie and let him know he wasn't going to win this battle.

Having saddled up another horse, he found Charlie with the saddle still on, and rounded him back up with the other team horses. Back at the main yard, Mike again climbed back up on Charlie and gave him a good workout. This time he was ready for every move Charlie made, daring him to repeat his previous performance. He didn't. One of the Weetman girls, Kay, used to ride him and get bucked off, but she always climbed back on so that he would not get in the habit of getting away with it. This was the secret to stop a horse from bucking.

Ted Weetman had another horse that needed breaking – a black Percheron mare called Lady. Charlie Isnardy had been trying to break this horse, and had spent a few days "sacking" him out.

One night after supper he asked Mike to give him a hand to hook Lady to a wagon, teaming her up with a gentle horse. Charley had his "running W" harness on the renegade mare, for good measure. This is a setup of two straps on each foot with a ring through which a rope goes through and up over the belly band to the driver. If the driver yanks on that rope, the feet are pulled out from underneath the horse, and obviously any high-speed run would terminate.

Ted said he would look after the running W and Mike could do the driving. Everything went along fine, and they drove all the way to the Carolan Place at Frost Creek. There they turned around and started back for home at the Pinchbeck Place. There was a sharp turn in the road, where Alvin Johnson's sawmill is today. At this turn the colt suddenly and without warning took off, and they were dealing with a runaway team.

Charlie Isnardy fell down and was lying in the bottom of the wagon; with the bouncing and jouncing, he was tossed about like popcorn in a pot. He could not get to his feet to operate the running W.

Mike was braced and hauling back on the reins with every bit of strength he possessed, but he was no match for the power of these four-legged locomotives who, at this point, did not care where they were headed, only that they were not going to stop going. He tried valiantly to steer them to the middle of the road and away from the dangers of the ditch and the trees on the side. They ran absolutely blindly, eventually plunging off the road, the wagon teetering precariously so that Mike and Charley were too preoccupied with hanging on to look for the running W rope. Into a copse of cottonwood trees they crashed, and came to a quivering stop as the harness and horses got tangled up around the trees, the wagon topsy-turvy against the roadside.

Charlie climbed up out of the wagon bottom "What in the hell are we doing down in the bush – why didn't you keep them on the road?" he yelled.

"I tried to," Mike panted, exhausted from the exertion, "Why didn't you pull your running W?"

"I tried to," retorted Charlie, "I fell down with your quick takeoff, when I got back to my feet, you were goin' too damn fast! I would have broken their necks if I would've pulled it then!" The running W would have pulled the feet out from underneath the horses – at the breakneck speed they were going, it would have been a disaster. The running W has to be used before getting up too much speed.

It was quite a time untangling everything, and coaxing the horses out of the bush. They were still jittery and agitated. The harness had to be put back together, and the horses had to be checked for injuries. They needed to be quieted down so that they could be hitched up to the wagon once more. The young black mare was still frothing from the experience, and refused

*Breaking Charlie*

to back up. She had to be maneuvered sideways and forwards until, little by little, they could persuade her to find an alternate way out of the bush.

Mike had to stay on the lines, guiding the horses; if they felt the least bit unattended, it was almost a certainty they would take off again. The wagon needed to be turned around in order to hitch the horses up to head in the proper direction. While Mike held tight control over the team, Charlie had to strain to pack the back end of the wagon around.

By the time they got back on the main road, darkness was falling. They headed back, the two men still leery and watchful, but the horses were too exhausted now to think about running away again.

The next night they took the same trip, not wanting to give the horse time to forget. They headed down the same hill. Sure enough, the same horse did the same thing at the same place. This time they were ready. At the first sign of trouble, Charlie pulled his running W rope, throwing the horse to its knees before she got going too fast. They had to do this a couple of times, until finally the horse was afraid to run, and was a much quieter team horse after that.

Runaways were commonplace in this era when young draft horses were constantly being trained, and springtime brought about the need for horses to be harnessed that had been idle for parts or all of the winter months. The draft horses had to be trained to back up, as it was not a normal motion for them.

Mike and working companion Richard Dick from the Alkali area had a large team of percherons hitched to a wagon one day to haul some rails out of the bush. This was a different sort of wagon, as it was flat and had no front side. They drove the team by simply standing on the flat rack. They had to travel down a slight incline and, as they did so, their load shifted forward, causing the front of the wagon to tip downwards. This caused both Mike and Richard to fall down on the shifting load and scramble for a handhold somewhere, as they were being dumped right onto the hind feet of the horses. As they slid down helplessly, rolling on the tumbling rails,

*Breaking Charlie*

both horses kicked back at them and sent them flying back up to the top of the wagon floor, only to start sliding down towards those huge kicking hooves again. There seemed to be no time to scramble out of the way, the horses were kicking at the rolling rails, and at them. They both got some memorable bruises before they managed to leap off, get the horses quieted down, and the wagon unloaded and back on the trail again. The load of timber had to be left behind.

Although they were stiff and sore and nursing various injuries, they laughed all the way back as they thought of the spectacle they must have made.

Men were thankful when they survived a runaway with no injuries to themselves or the horses, and not too much harness and equipment needing to be repaired afterwards.

Isadore Harry with Team Mulligan and Buster mowing Reed Canary grass at Alkali Lake Ranch

H. Krynen photo

Breaking Charlie

*Mike Isnardy cutting oats, Chimney Creek*        *Isnardy photo*

*Mike Isnardy cutting oats, Chimney Creek*        *Isnardy photo*

# Food from Heaven

## Chapter 9

1943 was a brutal endurance-testing winter – a record cold snap. The thermometer dipped from –40 to –60 below F for a period of six seemingly endless weeks. At the Mission School by Williams Lake, the students were told to stay in bed all day, as that was the warmest place in the huge but drafty building. It was impossible to keep the building warm enough to be comfortable.

Mike was working out in the Chilcotin, west of Williams Lake, cowboying on the C1 Ranch for Martin Duke and Jim Holt. It was in this area that his older sister Dorothy had met and married Alexis Creek resident Roy Haines. Mike had always wanted to know what it was like "out west" of Williams Lake.

Just west of this area, at Towdystan, where local Norwegian homesteader Harold Engebretson braved the harsh cold to get his and his wife Alyse's herd fed, the thermometer "separated" at –57 degrees, it was even too cold for the thermometer to register. The word Towdystan means "height of land" – in the Chilanko Forks area near the Dean River. Trading for furs was an established industry in this remote area, as the harsh climate was not suitable for growing produce to barter with on a shopping trip to the store. Prices paid for the furs ranged anywhere from twenty-five cents for a squirrel, to ten dollars for a prime coyote hide. Sometimes a lucky trapper would snare a silver fox, which would bring a thousand dollars in those days. A good-sized grizzly hide with the claws on could be sold for more than that.

This produced a particularly hardy population of settlers who survived by hunting and trapping, and using their wits to provide themselves with necessities. Harold built a spinning wheel for Alyce. They found the blueprints in the prairie newspaper "The Family Herald" and he used the wood from fruit packing boxes. He then spun the wool for her, and she in turn knitted countless sweaters, socks, hats, mitts and other articles that kept many people warm throughout the unforgiving and harsh winters.

There was a tendency towards a certain amount of lawlessness here that tested the faith and endurance of the early priests in the area. Harold Engebretson attended church one day to hear one particular preacher tell the members of his congregation that they were "the worst bunch of heathens he had ever seen."

Harold had originated in the Bella Coola area at the coast – his mother had packed him and his two siblings by horseback up the Palmer Trail to a place called Towdystan in the Anahim area to meet up with his father.

Settlers could buy land in this area for $1 to $3 per acre. The altitude was high – 3500 to 3700 feet above sea level. This developed a particularly hardy type of pioneer, as it was difficult to grow food, survival took forethought and endurance. Harold's mother once walked with another woman to the Bella Coola Store, twenty miles away, only to find the store closed and the owner not willing to open it. They walked all the way back without their much-needed supplies.

This prompted a local store to be opened up by the Christianson family. There was a store at Hanceville, closer to Williams Lake on the trail, that had been set up by Norman Lee, who came in the 1800's from England. There were many German and Scandinavian settlers in the area.

One particularly stocky German woman was in the Lee's Store on one occasion and wanted a hundred-pound sack of flour. These burlap sacks were tied with twine on the tops to appear to have "ears". When she was denied credit by storekeeper Mrs. Lee, the German woman grabbed the 100-lb sack by its "ear" with her thumb and one finger, and left with it. No-one dared to attempt to stop her.

Being out in these temperatures was downright dangerous, but hay had to be taken to the cattle and other animals, and waterholes had to be kept open for them to drink. Runners on the sleighs moved slower in the cold, extra time was needed for their chores; the massive work horses were allowed a much-needed rest every quarter mile. Mike Isnardy thought he was used to tough winter conditions, but found these frozen conditions a bit harsh and long-lasting for his liking.

After Christmas, Mike left the severity of the remote area out west, as he had now come to appreciate that the area he had been raised in was far more friendly as far as climate was concerned. He was also used to a closer community life, where the neighbours weren't situated quite so far away from each other.

He returned to the area south of Williams Lake, and found himself at the Diamond S Ranch at Dog Creek, nowadays called the Circle S. He started as a ranch hand, then choreboy, then cowboy. He remained there for three years, working for manager Frank Armes. Harold Armes was the foreman. There were twelve hundred head of calves on the feeding ground at the main ranch.

As the mercury in the thermometers hit bottom and refused to come back up, life became a full-time race to keep animals fed, watered and prevent them from freezing to death. The cowboys had to accomplish this without succumbing to the elements themselves. Frostbitten cowboys with scarves tied around their faces searched for new feeding areas in the timber that would offer some shelter from the wind; calves needed to be chased around to keep them moving, so they would not freeze on their feet. One team feeding could not keep up – an extra team had to be harnessed to try and keep up with the extra feed required to keep them alive; half-frozen calves stood around with their backs all humped-up against the harsh winter winds. The snow made cracking sounds under the sleigh runners.

A pale yellow sun hung back behind a frozen greyness, offering little in the way of warmth. Everywhere, the people withdrew from socializing, concentrating on the effort of getting through the conditions with as little loss as possible. No-one dared to leave their homes for any length of time, as the wood stoves needed to be constantly filled with firewood. Daylight hours were short, meaning that all the extra work had to be done in a smaller window of time.

Food from Heaven

Extra time and work were required for the heavy horse teams. The massive mounds of harness had to be hauled in where it was warm every night so they were not too frozen to be put back on the teams the next day. Those lucky enough to have barns left the horses standing in their harnesses all night, to eliminate the possibility of the harness becoming too stiff to put back on the following morning. The steel bits were removed from the bridles, so as not to freeze to the mouths of the horses.

The workhorses were fed extra rations, as more energy was needed to haul the massive amounts of feed to the cattle. Extra trips had to be made to watering holes to keep them open, as they froze over quickly, and the cows needed open water. Some of the watering holes were a mile or so away, and it took valuable extra time and stamina to get to them. Frostbitten cheeks, faces, fingers and toes were painfully commonplace.

The older cows were fed at the Pigeon Place, and some on the River Range. This particular winter Wycott Flats below the airport was rented from the Alkali Indian Band, which was an easier winter for the cows, and used the other ranges right down on the river, at Little Dog and Saul Pasture, between Little Dog and Wycott Flats.

WWII was still on, and the air force was making use of an airstrip they made at Dog Creek. As the bitter winter finally loosened its grip and the spring winds thawed the area, the army set up a temporary army barracks surrounding the airstrip. They even had a canteen, which proved most inviting for the neighbours. Weekends and Sundays in the summer found people from Alkali Lake and Dog Creek heading to the airstrip to play ball against the air force boys. They usually got badly beaten, but it was fun.

The Isnardy family was ever-changing. Alice came back from Alexis Creek to work at Alkali Lake Ranch, as housekeeper for the Reideman family, and got married to local Joe McLoughlin in 1944.

Although the older children in the family were out and about in the world, babies were still being born at the Isnardy home place.

Food from Heaven

In 1943 Frank came into the world, a little brother for them. He was only the second Isnardy baby that was actually born in the hospital. Although his older brothers and sisters were gone, he still had lots of siblings at home to teach him the routine of fitting into the household and farm. Geneva was four, Richard was six, Fred was seven, Olive was eight, Norman was ten, Rita was twelve, Amedee was fourteen, and Linda was fifteen. The twins Kenneth and Ronald were seventeen. Ken was out west working in the Chilcotin now. Alice and Mike were both away working. The older children from the first family were of course gone and busy with their own families – Tillie, Irene, James, Dorothy, and Andrew.

In the spring, attention had to be turned to readying the heavy horses for the upcoming haying season. Twenty or thirty horses were needed for haying. Some of these were only used at this time of year, so basically were wild horses for awhile, until any unruly notions had been worked out of them. There were no tractors, the sturdy horses did all the work. Along with their cowboying duties, the cowboys made time about a week before haying to hook the wild teams up to a wagon, and break them into the team routine, pairing up wild ones with gentle ones. They wanted any runaways to get bad habits out of their systems before the heavy working season began.

Using the rugged heavy horses for power was comfortable procedure for the able-bodied and capable men of this era. The giant horses needed training and upkeep (work horses needed to be fed well with good clean grain, green leafy hay, and grassy pasturelands) but proved their worth many times over in the days before machinery advanced onto the farms. Even after the gasoline-driven tractors came on the scene, the dependable working team horses proved to be easier to start and keep going in frigid temperatures. It was safer to use the draft horse teams on steep slopes than a tractor. On a muddy field, a good team would simply slog their way through, where a tractor would be stuck up to its axles. On a cold winter's day, you could climb up on a team horse and feel the warmth of his broad back beneath you – there is nothing warm or snugly about a tractor, and you wouldn't dream of climbing up and sitting on its frozen steel parts.

Although there were numerous runaways and some expected rebelliousness during training, for the most part these giant teams exhibited patience and a docile nature. There was always the added bonus of them naturally dropping fertilizer regularly on the fields upon which they worked. The men who worked with these horses were constantly on the lookout for breeding lines that had proven themselves in handling, size, and demeanor. News of a particularly good horse would travel very quickly and be a subject of great interest. When purchasing or trading for new team horses, the farmers generally followed the rule of "starting at the ground and working up", as of paramount importance was the condition of the horse's feet and legs, and the horse's ability to move quickly and confidently. It was known that you could train the top part of the horse, but it needed sound feet and legs upon which to build.

The greatest virtue of the draft horse era was that they kept life on a slower, even keel. It was good for the mind – with the added bonus of absence of diesel fumes – working with horses rather unnoticably kept life at an even tempo, as mankind geared himself to the slow and steady progress of the teams. It was a matter of pride to work behind a majestic pair of heavy horses that proudly picked their feet up in a good straight bouncing walk, their ears perked up attentively to the signals given by their driver.

Care had to be taken in the upkeep of the mountains of harness that went along with the business of using the draft horse teams. Harness that wasn't regularly cleaned and well oiled would become brittle and dry and apt to break with a sudden jerk. The result of this could spell disaster. Harness would be laid out in a warm place in "slack" time – a rainy day, or before spring work commenced. Necessary repairs would be made using a leather punch, rivets, an awl, and linen thread to redo loose stitches. Before warmed-up oil could be applied to the harness, dirt and sweat needed to be removed so the oil would be able to sink into the leather. They would use a sharp-edged piece of hard wood to scrape the harness as clean as possible before applying the oil.

Adjustments to harness size needed to be adhered to, as different teams were different sizes – in shoulder, girth, height, etc. Proper fit of collars, hames and harnesses prevented sore necks and shoulders on the animals. A poor-fitting harness, or one with a buckle rubbing on the wrong place, that caused discomfort to a team horse would greatly reduce its willingness to do heavy work. The work horses could normally pull twice their own weight.

The jingling of harness was a common occurrence, but not that handy if you were trying to be someplace without anyone knowing you were there. Local Lenny Derose about this time was working in the Soda Creek area for a widowed school teacher. When Lenny would show up on the team and sleigh with a load of hay for her cattle, this started a chain reaction.

The noisy jingling of the harness would start the cows to bawling; upon hearing the cows bawling, Stella would run out to give him suggestions or complaints, causing him to lose precious time to get the work done. Lenny overcame this problem by stopping his team before he got within earshot distance of her house. He would climb down from the wagon and wrap some gunny sacks around the noisy chain links of the harness, so there would be no jingling to start the cows bawling, and he could get the feeding done in peace.

Saddle horses needed to be broke, as well. Mike would break horses while cowboying. He got used to climbing on the new colts that had never been previously ridden – sometimes he took some terrible spills, but always managed to get back on to finish the job.

Getting bucked off a horse became a normal and routine occurrence for Mike Isnardy. He came to have very sharpened senses regarding green-broke and wild horses. He could get a feel about the way they acted, and whether they were "serious buckers" or ones that were simply trying to put forth a little bravado, then would settle down and communicate with the rider. He got better at being bucked off, meaning finding ways to fall that didn't hurt so much; to head off the horse in such a way that he would be more apt to land on his back end and feet, rather than his head or shoulders.

One balmy spring day on Dog Creek Mountain, the wind blew his hat off, and that was enough to spook the still half-wild colt he was riding. This small bay horse with a white blaze had never been halter-broke. Mike got off to pick up his hat, and when he attempted to get his foot in the stirrup to get back on, the jittery colt suddenly pulled away and took off, saddle and all. Mike chased after him on foot for a ways before he had to give up, the horse was going home without him. Norman Worthington, a long-time resident rider of the area, happened to find the colt and saddle back at the Dog Creek Mountain camp, with no Mike, and came looking to see if he had been hurt.

"Always halter break a colt before you ride him," was Norman's advice.

Moving the cattle around took in territory from Little Dog Creek, Airport, all the way through to the 70 Mile House area. Branding time happened at the Mountain Ranch, Pigeon Place, and Collins Lower Place. Horses needed to be branded as well – this was done at Mountain Ranch and Pigeon Place. They also needed to be shod – having steel horseshoes nailed on, so their feet didn't get sore on the rocky terrain.

It was usually Mike's job to shoe the colts for the first time. Blacksmith Joe Culmean with his big leather apron, had a place right on the Fraser River, across from Alkali Lake Ranch, but he was normally at his forge at Alkali, pumping the air into the forge to keep the fire hot, and fixing the shoes to fit each individual horse. This took a special talent, and although the cowboys attempted to pound the hot shoes to a proper fit, they never quite were able to accomplish this as effortlessly as Joe did.

Mike and the rest of the cowboy crew were sent to Gustafsen Lake, to move cows and calves out from the meadows in the spring to the summer range.

The herd didn't want to get started. The calves kept trying to go back to where they had come from, even though drift fences were built to stop them from going back. The cows were wanting to head in a different direction – to go to the spring range on the river. They would not wait for the calves, and Mike was attempting to keep the cows from leaving the calves behind. He was on Duke, a big bay horse. A group of cows headed out the wrong way and Mike galloped after them, trying to turn back the lead cow.

The long grass was coarse and dry and got wrapped around Duke's flying feet. Suddenly Duke pitched forward, and more forward, his feet tied up behind him in the rope-like grass. He went head over heels in a somersault, his rider underneath him. Duke scrambled shakily to his feet, empty saddle askew on his back; Mike lay motionless in the grass.

This is where he stayed until Norman Worthington came riding into the meadow, saw the cows all bunched up as though they had been driven, noted the riderless saddlehorse, and started looking around for Mike. He found Mike struggling to sit up in the grass, dizzy and disoriented.

The nearest place for assistance was Ray and Chrissy Pigeons, and Norman helped Mike onto Duke, and they began a slow ride to the Pigeon place. Mike remained there for about a week before he felt back to normal again.

The hay was poor at Holden Meadow. The cattle were thin – it took three days to move them, as they would play out and could only go a short distance every day. They would trail one day, then would have to leave them on the road the next day to rest. Mike and Ken had to haul hay in gunnysacks, from Collins Upper Place, about a ten mile ride, to feed the ones who were too weak to carry on with the others. They would fill two gunnysacks with hay, tie the sacks together and throw them over the back of the saddle.

Norman Worthington was the head rider. He was with them the first day to get all the strong cattle to Rollins Meadow. Then he left Ken and Mike to take the weak ones in and he rode back to the main ranch,

Food from Heaven

about thirty miles away.

When they had left the main ranch, Norman indicated they had sent grub supplies out for the two feeders, and the only thing they needed to take with them were their bedrolls. It was a day's ride from the main ranch to Holden Meadow. When Mike and Ken arrived there, the two feeders were there, Willie Billy from Dog Creek and Victor Lewis from Canoe Creek, but they were just about out of food.

There wasn't much left for breakfast the next morning. All the next day was spent moving cattle to Collins Meadow. There were five riders in total – Mike, Ken, Norman, and the two feeders, Willie and Victor, and all they had to eat was flour. They mixed up flour and water, and baked it. It was pretty hard chewing but it did fill up their growling stomach cavities.

The next morning, they had the same thing for breakfast. Norman and Victor left and went back to the main ranch, promising that Victor would return right away with food for Mike and Ken. He never did show up.

Mike was doing the cooking. One meal he mixed flour and water together, and cooked it up; the next meal he chuckled as he told Ken and Willy he was changing the recipe – to water and flour.

This went on for three days. They were all getting thinner and thinner, and were noticeably losing weight. Their days were filled with hard work, there was no time for hunting or fishing – at night they had nothing to eat. Breakfast was an important meal to these hardworking cowboys – Mike was used to eating a hearty and substantial helping of eggs, bacon, and hotcakes with Rogers Golden syrup from a pail. The flour and water was a poor substitute, as they watched hopefully for Victor or anyone to appear with some rations.

Even their flour was running out now, and after they got the cattle moved in to Collins Meadow, Ken and Mike took off, leaving Willie Billy alone to feed the three hundred and fifty head of cattle. They were starving, and losing precious energy and strength as each rationless day went by. By now they had given up any

Food from Heaven

hope that Victor was going to show up with supplies.

It was a beautiful crisp day and, despite their growling hungry bellies, they were laughing and enjoying the newness of early spring, and joking about how their belts were running out of notches to tighten up.

About ten miles down the road, Mike noticed something strange by the side of the road. Riding closer, they discovered to their profound delight that it was a large chunk of bologna, still in the wrapper. Half the bologna roll was still frozen in the snow, the upper part sticking up invitingly and thawing out in the sun's rays.

Mike looked towards the heavens, as he figured that was the only answer to the confounding coincidence that these two starving brothers would just happen upon this beautiful big roll of bologna out in the middle of nowhere. A further miracle was that it had not been found by coyotes, wolves, or the like. Never had anything looked or tasted so good. They were so hungry, they ate about half of it, relishing every morsel. Then they stuck what was left back up in the snow for some other hungry fellow.

Another ten miles of riding brought them to the Pigeon Place. Ray and Chris Pigeon and their family always made them welcome, and served up a good homecooked meal of roast beef with all the trimmings, topped off with wild blueberry pie. It was a miracle that Ken and Mike didn't founder themselves eating.

They headed back to the main ranch with their bellies full and satisfied, and met Victor Lewis about a half mile before they got to the Ranch. His pack horse was loaded down with food for him and Willy Billy.

"What happened to our food?" Mike asked.

"Oh, I went on a li'l toot," grinned Victor.

"Well, Willy's getting pretty hungry out there, the flour's all gone," Mike said.

"Oh, hell, he's Indian, he'll make out," Victor retorted with a grin.

Everyone had a big laugh, and headed about their way.

A month or so later when Mike ran into Willy Billy, he asked him how he made out with no food.

He replied that he had trapped some muskrats, so had plenty to eat.

Norman Worthington &
Mike Isnardy, Diamond S,
Dog Creek 1942 Isnardy photo

Quin Able, Mike Isnardy,
Norman Worthington,
Diamond S Ranch, Dog Creek

James, Evelyn and Dorothy with Dorothy's family, Alexis Creek

Food from Heaven

# Cattle Drives

L ife for the ranchers and their cowboys was a constant effort of moving the animals to proper grazing areas, making sure that no specific area was over-grazed. They had to be driven to market, sometimes to the railway. Rain, shine, snow, wind, or hail, even the deaths of important people, did not stop these very necessary drives.

Mike participated in drive after drive. In early spring, two drives of steers were taken to Pavilion Mountain, with two herds of cows (about three hundred and fifty head) and calves brought back. Each way took about two weeks. Twelve riders herded the cows, and one fellow drove extra horses, so the cowboys would have fresh transportation when their horses tired. A three-ton truck hauled the little calves that became too tired to keep up. They were still pretty small, in fact some were born on the drive.

After the calves had ridden on the truck during the day, they had to be matched up with their mothers for feeding at the end of the day's ride. It was always a challenge to match the calves to the right mother, sometimes they had to just rope a cow with a full bag, and allow a calf to suck, whether it was the right mother or not. In the morning they would look for any calves that appeared weak and hungry, and rope a cow for them to suck before the day's journey began. Many of the calves developed scours, a diarrhea condition that proved fatal for some of them.

A cook and a chuckwagon accompanied this outfit. Moffatt Jack was the cook. The chuckwagon was basically a large wagon with no top.

On one particular cattle drive, it rained heavily the first night – everyone's bedrolls got wet; with no way to dry them. This turned out to be the first of many wet and miserable nights for them. The rain didn't stop, so the bedrolls never got a chance to dry out.

Four or five cattle drives to Williams Lake were made

towards the end of the season. When the cattle drives made their way into Williams Lake, it was cause for celebration as the long trek was over. There would be warm bath water, clean clothes, drinks at the local tavern, music, ladies, and time for socializing before heading out of town again. This was when much bartering and trading deals were accomplished, for notable horseflesh or a particular bull with a good breeding reputation. The cowboys were always ready to "let loose" after long hard days and nights on the trail pushing cattle in to their destination, the auction. They looked forward to letting their hair down and downing their share of whiskey before leaving town. Mike was a seasoned cattle drive hand, and he and his partners relished the socializing that accompanied the completion of a cattle drive to market.

A disaster preceded one particular cattle auction day. The local liquor board store burned to the ground sometime during the night before. As the sun rose in the sky on the day of the auction, there were only smoking remnants of the building that would have been the site of frenzied activity later on in the day when riders, ranchers and buyers finished with their auction duties.

A large truck served as a temporary liquor store following the fire. When the thirsty cowboys trailed in to the auction, news of the fire spread and, fearing that all the whiskey would be gone before the sale ended, they hurriedly pooled their money and made a list of their needs.

Alkali Lake cowboy Hank Krynen was delegated to head to the liquor truck and buy their "supplies" before they ran out.

Hank took off in Red Allison's '49 Chevrolet pickup, with an impressive wad of money to pay for the truckload of booze for his thirsty cowboy companions.

Back at the stockyards, the return of the truck was met with shouts of glee. On normal sale days, the work was all done before the drinking started. On this day, everyone rushed to retrieve their orders, and of course, no-one was saving it until later.

Ray Pigeon and George Felker were running the

sale, and they tried valiantly to keep order. The sale progressed in fine fashion. Signs with pen numbers were normally stapled to the gates – there were now cowboys riding around with these signs stapled on their backs; one cowboy made a boasting swoop from his horse and toppled off into the dust; another rider attempted to lassoo one of the spectators.

Somehow the sale was accomplished, and a rousing time was had by all, certainly an auction to remember.

Except for one intoxicated old cowboy, who woke up all by himself in the alleyway near the local hotel the following morning. He sat up, squinting in the brightness of the early sunshine, not sure just where he was, or how he had gotten there.

He eyed his dented cowboy hat lying in the dirt, picked it up, beat some of the dust out of it, and crammed it onto his head. Struggling shakily to his feet, he headed towards the corner of the building to the main street.

Something didn't feel quite right, he felt breezy and loose. Looking down at his now-wrinkled shirt and wellworn chaps, he shook his head in confusion at the scuffed-up condition of his previously shined-up cowboy boots. For the life of him, he couldn't remember what had happened to mess them up so.

Slowly and deliberately, he made an unsteady entry into the café around the corner for a cup of coffee. He paused at the door, swiping some dried grass from the front of his shirt and trying his best to pull himself together in as presentable a fashion as possible. He felt briefly at the belt of his chaps to make sure all was intact.

Although the café was crowded, he saw no familiar faces, and proceeded towards an empty table.

Suddenly the Chinese owner of the café glimpsed him and immediately began pointing at him and yelled "Get him out of here!"

All conversation halted as the bewildered cowboy was ousted by the excited Chinaman dragging him towards the exit, still yelling "Out – Out – you gettie dlessed to come in here!" Laughter and hooting from the other patrons echoed in his ears as the door shut behind him, the angry Chinaman standing defiantly with his arms crossed on the other side to prevent any re-entry plans he might have had.

He began to study himself to scrutinize just what the problem could be. Now he looked around his backside where there seemed to be air blowing freely through his jeans. Startled, he twisted around to see further, as there didn't appear to be any jeans there, only his underwear. Feeling with his hands now, he backed up against the wall of the building, his mind searching for an answer as to where his pants were.

Someone had gone to the trouble of removing his pants, and then had put his chaps back on overtop of his underwear. He made a quick retreat along the building, his back towards the wall all the way, until he could escape into the alley again.

On another such "end of the trail" day, the Hargreaves outfit from the Soda Creek area herded their cattle into town, straight up the main Oliver Street. On the next street over, Fred Kozuki was just putting the finishing touches to a new cement sidewalk.

Fred and his wife Lily were one of the first Japanese families to reside in Williams Lake following the upheaval of the Japanese evacuation from the coastal areas during WWII. They came to town with nothing but their children, as all their possessions, business and property had been taken away from them. It wasn't long before everyone recognized them as hard-working delightful people, who refused to harbour any bitterness over the assets they had lost, and the abysmal treatment they had endured.

Now Fred stood back and rather proudly surveyed how smooth the surface of the new cement was. He had toiled on it since the early light of dawn; now all he had to do was wait for it to harden and dry.

He was vaguely aware of the cattle drive that was heading down Oliver Street. He heard the lowing and moo-ing of some of the cows, and heard the odd "hi-ya" from the cowboys, and slapping leather sounds.

Suddenly there seemed to be a different kind of commotion, as a number of the lead animals spooked and headed down the street where Fred stood. Most of the cowboys were at the back of the herd, and the front riders could not stop the rest of the stampeding animals from following the lead renegade runaways. They headed straight for Fred's new cement sidewalk.

For a few harrowing moments he stood in their path, valiantly waving his arms, jumping up and down and yelling, trying to steer them away from his freshly finished but still glistening-wet cement project. He was finally forced to leap for safety, as he realized the pounding masses of horns and flying hooves would trample him down into the cement if he stayed. He watched helplessly as they stampeded over his new cement sidewalk, flying chunks of mud-like concrete splattered past him. In hot pursuit of the fleeing cattle galloped the cowboys, their horses' sharp shod hooves pounding through the now pulverized remnants of his doomed sidewalk.

Mike and his fellow cowboys thoroughly enjoyed the goings-on in the town at the end of the drives. They laughed and joked, made deals and trades, danced and ate and drank, started relationships and ended relationships – it was a wild time, and they loved it. Before they left town, they had to remember to load up the pack horses. In the winter, they carried as much coarse salt as possible; in the summer it was rock salt, to be hauled back out to the ranching outfits.

The last drive was three hundred and fifty head of steers, cows, and bulls. It was late fall and the trail started at Pigeon Place and carried on through U.S. Meadows. The cowboys camped there in an early heavy wet snow. This was when cowboying was not fun, nor romantic. They were cold, miserable and wet. Their boots also became soaked. At night they had to pull their boots off to dry their feet – the next day it was nearly impossible to get the boots back on their feet again.

Henry Able drove a 3/4 ton Fargo truck with the camping gear. There was no antifreeze in it, which resulted in the block freezing up. The next day he had to keep filling it with water to make it as far as Springhouse. Antoine and May Boitano lived there, descendants of Augustin Boitano, who was the original owner of the land where the settlement of Springhouse was established. He had come to the area in 1858 running a pack train, and followed similar employment until 1914.

At Boitano's place, the chuckwagon and team headed back to Dog Creek, while the crew forged ahead. Pinchbecks lodged six cowboys that night, before they carried on to Williams Lake. When the drive started by the airport, they stayed the first night at Little Dog Creek, then owned by Diamond S; the next day they made it as far as Alkali Lake; the next night to Boitanos at Springhouse; the next night at Pinchbecks, then on to Williams Lake, arriving there early in the day.

One spring Ken and Mike drove one carload of steers to Kelly Lake. They left Dog Creek as spring was coming, the ground was bare, and the grass was starting to grow. They camped the first night at the Koster Ranch at Canoe Creek, the next night at Indian Meadows, then on to Harry Marriott's OK Ranch; on to the Mountain Ranch owned by Pete Coldwell, then ended up at Kelly Lake, where they herded the steers on to the rail car.

They weren't finished then – they headed on to Pavilion to pick up some horses, six head saddle horses, and one Arabian stud to drive back to Dog Creek. There was still snow at Pavilion, and the feeding was still being done with sleighs. Clarence Bryson was managing the Pavilion outfit, although it was owned by Diamond S. The trip back with the horses only took two days, as they travelled much faster than cows, and of course there were no straggling weak calves to worry about.

The following spring Frank Armes bought some thirty Hereford breeding bulls and brought them to Meadow Lake. Mike and Ken stayed at Rose Pigeon's there, then drove the bulls on to Tom Patton's place on Gustafsen Lake, which had been sold to the Diamond S. Victor Lewis was herding bulls for the Diamond S at this prime meadow location.

Here they put the two bunches of bulls together and

did not get any sleep as the bulls fought and bawled all night. The next day, they separated the sparring bulls, and eventually turned them out to range where they could settle their pecking order problems at their leisure.

U.S. Cow Camp

Chuckwagon U.S. Cow Camp

Cattle Drive, OK ranch, 1944

Cattle Drive (Mike holding hands up) 1944

A ntoine Boitano was Mike Isnardy's hero. Antoine's father Augustine Boitano left Italy in the early 1830's, landing up in Philadelphia, and eventually following the gold-luring stories to Canada in the early 1880's.

Antoine was born in 1885, and grew up helping his father with his pack train business. He owned what was known as the Springhouse Ranch until 1942, (today the ClarkTucker ranch). It bordered the Fraser River; there was a store and a Post Office, and it was a hub of activity, there was even a saloon, with music and dancing. Horse races were a favorite pastime, and the flat along the lake became the race track. Part of this property was sold to the Alkali Lake Ranch.

Antoine followed his father's lead and became a tough and capable handler of horses and pack mules, becoming something of a legend in the area for his packing abilities. Although he was a rough and tough chaser of wild horses (they would catch them, break them, and then sell them to the army during the war), he also had a softer side - he was a fiddle player, and a quiet humble soft-spoken gentleman.

In his early twenties, an encounter with a cantankerous old mule left a horrific memory for Antoine. They had been chasing the wild horses, and had separated a large strong-looking mule from the rest of the herd, thinking that he had the makings of a good pack horse. They were constantly on the lookout for animals that were strong enough to carry heavy loads.

In an attempt to brand and halterbreak this wild mule, Antoine tackled his front legs and tried to hogtie them. The mule lunged and grabbed Antoine by the ankle. Antoine's unrestrained screams of pain brought all other activities to a halt, as the rest of the crew rushed to his aid. They converged on the maniacal mule with his jaws firmly clamped around Antoine's bloodied leg. The mule's eyes were wild, rolling around trying to see everything around him, but his mouth remained as though welded shut.

They pounded on the mule, they pulled his ears, they poked and kicked him, hoping that he would release his grip on the ankle to rear up at them. Nothing, absolutely nothing would break the mule's hold on the lad's leg. Desperation began to set in, as more blood poured from the wound, and they began to worry about shock and infection.

"Shoot 'im," someone yelled. This seemed like the only solution to get rid of the mule. When they thought further about this tactic, they became worried that the death throes might make the mule's teeth grind even harder into Antoine's flesh.

Antoine's brother Lawrence finally ran to get a crowbar. Leaping back into the corral, he knelt by the mule's head and the gruesome bleeding mess that was Antoine's lower leg. As gently as he could, he levered the crowbar into the mule's mouth beside Antoine's shattered ankle. Firmly and doggedly, he pried the jaw until it loosened enough that they could pull the injured leg out.

The anklebone was clearly crushed, and Antoine was carried away to safety, to await the arrival of a doctor summoned from 150 Mile. The doctor arrived, examined the leg, and cleaned the wound as best he could. Shaking his head gravely, he then gave them an alarming verdict, breaking the news to them that they could possibly expect infection, blood poisoning, perhaps resulting in the loss of the leg. This was a very serious injury.

His grim predictions partially came true – infection did set in, blood poisoning wracked the young man's system with pain and high fevers. Augustine turned to his women friends from Alkali to use their native herbs and medicines to help his son.

It was over a year before Antoine eventually recovered. He married the devoted young nurse who cared for him during this time, May Hamilton. They had one daughter, Chrissy.

Chrissy grew up and married local rancher Ray Pigeon, and 1946 found Mike working on their spread called the Old Goodrich Place.

There was no end of work, but the work was changing. They branded animals, broke horses, fed cattle, cut wood, rails, cleaned ditches, irrigated, and picked rocks.

The change was that the big lumbering steady workhorses were being replaced with machines. Feeding was done by tractor and sleigh, there was no longer any need for the teams. Horses were turned loose by the droves, becoming wandering and flourishing wild horse herds. Ranchers did not want to keep horses that needed to be fed and looked after, when they were no longer used for work. Trucks and tractors were now used to haul grain and hay. Fred Mellish hauled grain for heifers; Hodgsons went into the business of hauling cattle by truck – this brought an end to the romance and adventure of the cattle drives.

Other labor-saving devices and machines were fast hitting the market. Cross-cut saws were being replaced with chainsaws, the most popular was the Wade Grey saw. Ray had a Ferguson tractor now which performed the ploughing and discing duties.

Mike still did harrowing with the horses, and still picked rocks with a team and wagon.

The horses used here were a large percheron team called Molly and Star. Molly was part Clydesdale. Ray did the mowing with the tractor, and Mike did the raking. The hay still needed to be stacked, and the sloops were still put into action. Mike would load them with the team in the field, Ray would haul them in to stack with the tractor, using two sloops. Antoine was the stacker.

The next year, Ray got a buck rake for his tractor, and would back the hay into the stack. He could then put the hay on slings and pull it up into a stack with the tractor. Mike did the stacking. This saved one man.

The Pigeon family all went to Vancouver for a holiday, and Mike had the place, and the work, all to himself. After the work was under control, riding the range and branding a few late calves, he would go deer hunting with Antoine. Antoine loved hunting, he was especially lucky, or skilled, at goose hunting around Axe Lake and Colpit Lake. Once, at Springhouse, he got nine geese with two shots from his shotgun.

In the fall, Ray bought a bunch of yearling heifers at a sale in Williams Lake. That winter there was an outbreak of coccidiosis, and it was necessary to doctor the calves with sulpha. They pulled their tongues out, dropped the oblit as far back in their mouths as they could, then let their tongues loose, the backwards movement of the tongue would make the pill fall down their throats. Ted Cornwall, the local Agriculturist, sent samples away to determine if they had the illness or not.

Mike built a garage for Ray from logs, which was laborious axe-work. He cut the fir trees down with an axe and peeled the bark from them. The roof was fashioned from peeled poles laid side by side, then covered with a layer of hay, followed by dirt on top of the hay. It was a nice warm building, as it had a heater in it. One end was for chickens. Two cows needed to be milked. He walked to where the Chimney Creek School is now to fetch them, then milked them and separated the milk.

There were still young horses to break, and Mike worked with a white-faced black colt called Skiezik. After he had it gentle and broken to halter, he led the horse around with Jim Pigeon on it. One day it crow-hopped around and young Jim was just about falling off. Although Mike got hold of him and saved him from hitting the ground, his mother Chrissie was looking out of the window, and told him never to put him on again.

The next day Ray and Chris went to town and Mike saw his chance to get Jim back on Skiezik. This time there were no problems, and both the boy and the horse were happy.

They built a new root cellar out of the old one, as the aged logs were beginning to rot and needed to be replaced with new ones. Mike used to watch moose feeding around on the hillside across from the house in the mornings in the winter. He shot his first moose right from the house, and dragged it by himself into the windlass. This was simply a winch-like device that was built to hang the carcass up off the ground. Two poles were erected about 8' apart, four sticks were used on the crosspart to pull the rope around to raise the

The Stampede Parade, Williams Lake, BC

Williams Lake, Cariboo, BC

James Isnardy with 5 of the children
Richard, Norman, Rita, Fred, Ollie and James

Evelyn with Curly and Sonny

Linda and Alice

Ken, Mike, Norman
and Steve Frizzi

Fred, Frank and Ollie at Springhouse

Springhouse area                                    H.Krynen photo

Springhouse homestead

Springhouse homestead

*Alkali lake and surrounding area*                    *H.Krynen photo*

*Saddlehorses ready to work*

Springhouse School

Church on wheels Sunday school truck

Frank in front of house, Frost Creek

Cow camp at Williams Lake

Cowboy Red Allison getting rid of some trail dust          Earl Chill photo

Cowboys Hank Krynen and Red Allison, team ropers

Hank Krynen and Bill Twan at Dog Creek Dance
photo by Al Becker, courtesy of Robert Becker

John Rosette, Alkali Lake, 1965

H.Krynen photo

*Harold Engebretson in a fiddling mood*

*Long-time ranchers Sue and Chow Lee*

Ray (Raybone) Johnson, Alkali cowboy. Died 1996    H.Krynen photo

Cowboy Hank Krynen, hauling hay

Stacking bales at Alkali, Isadore Harry, Clifford Dan and Sam Wycotte
H.Krynen photo

Mike Isnardy and Gil Bowe bulldogging at Courtenay

Cowboy Sellars eating dust (horse is Snip)          Art Long photo

Mike Isnardy, wild cow milking

Warren Brass gives Ol' Come Apart a try          H.Krynen photo

Mike Isnardy, pick up man, Goodrich Place          H.Krynen photo

Hopeful cowboy Rod Rimmer on Simon                    T.Engebretson

Cowboy takes his chances on a wild bull-ride          Tommys rodeo pictures

Mike Isnardy and Barb Bowser, Williams Lake Stampede Parade, 1992

Mike and sister Alice

carcass. This device was also put to use when beef cattle were butchered.

The Pigeon kids each had a horse – Jim had a sometimes-balky little pony called Pennie that Antoine and May got from Patty Cripps, one that Jim Harris and Cherry used to ride when they were little. Terry used to ride Ranger, and Marie would ride Funny Face.

One day Marie and Jim were riding up along the river above Chimney Creek when they found a coyote den. They carried a shovel with them the next day and dug out the coyote puppies and brought them home for pets. Marie put on heavy gloves when she played with them, as they nipped a bit. She tried to tame them, but they became increasingly meaner, and after a couple of months they had to be turned loose.

It was here that Mike experienced another runaway with the team. He headed out to get a load of hay with the sleigh hitched up to a team called Star and Blackie. Blackie was substituting for a horse called Molly, who was recuperating from a lame leg. On the way back to the barn, with a full load of hay, they took off without warning, and nothing would hold them back. Mike finally stopped pulling back on the reins and just let them run until they tired and couldn't run anymore. At least there were no trees to crash into this time. He felt lucky to come out of it virtually unscathed, and the sleigh and harness still in one piece.

In 1948 Mike went to work as a faller, with Amedee for a partner, for a sawmill by the name of Soule Bros. at Springhouse. Ike Soule was the boss, a hard-working and enjoyable guy. They worked as a team, falling trees with a cross-cut saw – it was a daunting task to be able to cut logs fast enough to keep the mill going. Dave Pierce had an old Hornet chain saw he lent to them, it would run for an hour or so and then it would quit. They would then go back to the reliable cross-cut saw. It took two men to run the chainsaw – one man would hold a stem on the end of the cutting bar and the other would run the saw.

"T – I-M-B-E-R", yelled Mike, as he stepped back from the falling tree. Nobody was expected to be

Mike's Hero

around. Just then he saw two cowboys coming – Pete Rasmussen and Bob Sonberg, hot on the tail of a bull. By now it was too late to even yell again, as the tree crashed close to the bull. Luckily, Pete had heard the "timber" call and stayed back.

This summer was a wet one, the rains fell relentlessly, and the clay-dirt logging road became a quagmire. They hauled loads of rocks to dump on the swampy road, but they soon sank out of sight. The rocks were big, as large as they could handle, and all had to be lifted in the truck by hand. After falling trees all day, Mike would help Gilbert Bowe move sawdust back from the mill with the team and a big scoop made out of lumber. The sawdust piled up around the saw, and had to be removed so that it wouldn't plug up the mill.

Later they gave Mike a contract falling trees at Frost Creek, as he had a timber sale there. Amedee and Mike stayed at their old home. Mike bought a team, in addition to using their father's team, and they went to work falling, then skidding with the two teams. They never got paid their final payment for these logs, as the mill went broke.

The mill had two teams skidding in the bush. Alice's husband, Joe McLouchlin, was using the big team, weighing about 1700lbs. Ivan Bowe was using a team of roans weighing about 1400lbs. They used them to cross-haul. This was done by tying a chain to the frame of the truck back across the top of the deck of the truck, then a long cable with a hook on the end was put around the log, and back to the chain. When the team on the other end of the cable pulled, the log rolled up onto the truck. If the log started to go crooked, there was a man there with a peavie to grab the end that was getting behind. He would hook the log and pull ahead a little until the log straightened out on the truck. There were two skids, one end on the ground, and the other end on the truck.

There was lots of work, it was never totally finished, but they always had time for joking and clowning around. One of the fellows asked Mike –

Mike's Hero

"what is that thing that goes under the horses tail?"
Mike wanted to be fast at answering questions, and
was happy that he knew the answer.

"It's a crooper," he quickly replied.

This was exactly what the guy was waiting for – "Any
horse's ass knows that!" he replied, to the raucous
laughing of everyone around.

When a particular portion of the work was done,
there would be the party at the Maple Leaf Hotel, owned
by Benny Abbott. They used to rent a room with four
beds, four loggers to a room. This was their time to let
off steam, to laugh and joke, and to enjoy the company
of ladies. It was here that Mike first met a sawyer by the
name of George – a big raw-boned Swede, weighing
around two hundred pounds. He turned out to be one
of the kindest guys around, and was willing to help with
anything in the events of the working days.

The old Maple Leaf Hotel was a rocking establish-
ment in those years, for the cowboys, loggers, and
other crews that needed to let off steam after a cattle
drive, or other events. Much good-time jostling,
partying, and wild rampages went on. It wasn't the
place to go if you wanted a good night's sleep.
Sometimes furniture and items that belonged in the
rooms were found out on the street the following
morning. Nobody, of course, knew how they got there.

Benny Abbott got used to dealing with all manner of
bizarre goings-on within the confines of his establish-
ment, one of the strangest being a cowboy riding his
horse right into the bar one night.

There was much bragging about the appaloosa
stud named Cheamo that had recently come from
Alberta; local cowboy Mickey Martin wanted to show
off this stallion's merits and rode him right into the
bar of the Maple Leaf Hotel.

Benny Abbott kept his cool, as the handsome
horse pranced around amidst the hooting patrons.
Finally he thought of a way to get them out without
causing any more upheaval. "How old is that horse?"
he yelled.

"Six years," answered Mickey, from the back of the

horse. He pulled back on the reins to cause Cheamo to rear up, just for effect.

"Sorry," replied Benny, "you have to be twenty-one to come in here. He'll have to leave!"

*James Isnardy and Joe McLaughlin*

*Mike's Hero*

# Potato King

## Chapter 12

In August of 1948, Sid Pigeon made a proposal to Mike Isnardy, as they relaxed over a beer in the Maple Leaf Hotel. He and Doc Avery had just purchased the Chimney Creek Ranch from the Buckley brothers, Jerry and Dan, who had made the decision to move to Kelowna to go into the motel business, the Kelowna Comfy Club.

"We're going to grow potatoes," Sid claimed, "Lots of potatoes! We need someone to run the place – are you interested?"

Mike was taken by surprise. He was twenty-five years old and had worked with cattle, horses, all manner of other farm animals, haying equipment, ploughing, fencing; milking, weeding gardens, had done his share of work with the raspberries, currants, etc., in the garden, picked wild strawberries – heck, he had even tried his hand at growing peanuts. But he had never grown a whole farm full of potatoes.

"I don't know anything about growing potatoes!" he told Sid.

"Oh, we'll help with the potatoes," offered Sid, "all the other ranch work needs to be done as well – we can hire people when we need them for the potatoe work."

Mike was game for anything and was always interested in new enterprises, and Sid's enthusiasm was contagious. He took the job on. He moved to the Chimney Creek Ranch, which would now be called the A&P Ranch, when the Buckley brothers moved to Kelowna in late fall.

Mike's first priority was to get the fields ploughed up in preparation for planting the potatoes the next spring. The hay crop belonged to A&P with the deal, and it was sold to local ranchers Charlie and Pudge Moon.

Pudge Moon's ancestry was English, he was named Rexford Albion Moon at his birth. As he was a chubby little baby, the name Pudge seemed a much more suitable name, and stuck with him his entire life.

Pudge had his own experience with a runaway team. His son, also named Rexford (Rex) and his daughter Lillian, who grew up to marry B.C. Hydro employee Don Fletcher, were young and searching for excitement one day.

The heavy horse team was harnessed to a wagon and standing idle in front of the house. Rex and Lillian decided to don themselves in two bearskins that they knew were in the shed, just to see what the horses would do if they saw two bears.

They ran to the shed and emerged a few minutes later, each covered with a black bear skin. They headed to where the unsuspecting team stood peacefully, seemingly dozing on their feet. Rex and Lillian got down on their hands and knees and crept closer and closer, trying to move as bears would.

When they ambled into the horses' view, reaction was swift and immediate. The team took off without any hesitation whatsoever. Like stones shot from a slingshot, they plowed over everything in their path, racing blindly away from the now-frightened "bears" who could only stand helplessly and watch the chaos they had initiated.

A wooden outhouse stood directly in the team's path. The fleeing team were running blindly and crashed right into it and overtop of it, demolishing the two-seated structure, boards and toilet paper and magazines flying in every direction.

Pudge by now was out of the house, a half-eaten sandwich still in his hand. He tore after the horses, wondering all the while what could possibly have set them off like that. He had visions of broken harness and wagon, perhaps injuries to the team and, most crucial of all, it was obvious that the family now had no privy.

This team was used by the haying crew, for hauling the bundles of straw that were left after the monstrous belt-driven threshing machine separated the straw from the grain in the field. The sweating men on the threshing crews toiled under the merciless sun, to beat any forecasts of impending rain.

One young fellow on such a crew lost his pack of cigarettes and matches from his shirt pocket as he leaned over the machine. The thresher chewed them up

Potato King

on their way through, and the matches were ignited. As the straw spewed out the back end, wisps of smoke accompanied it, which then burst into a wholehearted blaze as the air flamed it.

"Fire!!!" one of the men finally yelled, pointing to the burning straw pile. The fire was quickly spreading to the dry crop that was all around. All hands left what they were doing, and converged on the burning mass. There was no water in the immediate vicinity and to wait for some to arrive would take too long. Someone grabbed a good-sized tarp that was on the thresher and yanked it off. Positioning themselves on all sides, they pulled it over the top of the fire, holding the edges down to smother the flames.

Their strategy worked; starved for air, the fire died.

Mike started to feed Moon's cattle in the winter. They were bringing more cattle to be fed, and Mike could not continue this work, as he had to start making wooden sprouting boxes for the potatoes. Willie Crosina, a single cowboy who would later marry Terry Pigeon, was hired to take over the winter feeding job for the A&P.

Willie's father was Louis Crosina, who operated the store at 153 Mile, and a blacksmith shop for the teamsters that passed through on a steady basis. The original barn, blacksmith shop, store, and log house are still standing there today as a heritage reminder, owned by the Patenaude family.

Mike started building the sprouting boxes in the dining room of the house. They had to be specific – two feet wide, three feet long, six inches high on the ends, but only four inches high on the sides, to allow room for a watering can to water. Sand was placed in the bottom of each box, then the cut seed potatoes, topped with more sand. The boxes were then stacked one on top of another about five feet high. They had to be kept moist, so that the seed potatoes would not dry up and shrivel.

Forty-five gallon barrels were wrestled into the house so they would be watered with warm water. Mike packed in water from the well to fill these barrels, two five-gallon buckets at a time. It was a full-time job just keeping them from drying out over the winter months.

Potato King

Mike could hardly wait for spring, so he could move them all outside and get them planted into the ground.

April rolled around, with the promise of a good growing summer to follow. A tobacco planter had been purchased to plant the mountain of sprouted seed potatoes. The planter made a single ditch, and two people sat on the back of the machine, close to the ground, sticking a potato in the ground by hand, carefully, to ensure the fragile sprouts didn't break off. The machine covered the potatoes with soil from each side. Sid Tressiera drove the tractor, while Mike and Bert Johnson planted the tubers. They sat on the machine and carefully stuck them down into the soil, first one from Mike, then one from Bert, back and forth, day after bending-down day.

At times Ken would come and spell Mike off so he could look after the other chores on the ranch. It was necessary to run two shifts on one tractor for the other spring ploughing. Amedee Isnardy started early in the morning, Ken would then take over in the middle of the afternoon and work until darkness stopped him. The early potatoes were planted in April, down by the river where spring came early, in an area called Moores' Truck Garden. In this fashion they got all the potatoes in the ground – seven acres of early potatoes (ones that would be harvested in June) and forty acres planted in May for the fall harvest.

Two huge hoppers were filled with cut potatoes for the forty acre planting. An actual potato planter had been purchased for this monumental job. Four natives from the Toosie Reserve had been hired to cut the potatoes into seed. The two planters were able to sit much higher on this machine, making it more comfortable with more room for their legs to hang down. They didn't have to bend down to plant the potatoes either, they merely had to watch that the potatoes did not get jammed up in the round table with holes drilled a certain distance apart. Only one potato was supposed to be in each hole; if there were more, the person had to grab one off and throw it back into the hopper.

The potatoes were taking up a lot of time. Haying,

irrigating, ploughing the fields on the rest of the ranch had to be kept up at the same time. Water for irrigating came from Brunson Lake, Chimney Lake, and Felker.

Dams on these lakes controlled the flow of water coming down, and sometimes people would tamper with the dams, shutting off the water so desperately needed below. To travel to these lakes to remedy this problem meant a day's ride on horseback. If they tried to shorten this trip by taking a pickup truck, they risked getting stuck on the poor roads and wasting more valuable time.

These were busy days that flew by in a blur of activity. The crew of Bert Johnson (and his wife May, who came to cook), Sy, Kenny, Amedee, and Mike worked from sunup until as late in the day as their eyes could see. They managed to keep ahead of the weeding and irrigating of the potatoes, and still kept the other ranch work going.

Then came time to harvest the potatoes. The oblong good-sized potatoes were ploughed out of the ground, and ten natives from Sugarcane Reserve were hired to pick them up from there into one hundred pound burlap sacks. At first they were being paid by the day, and this was a pretty slow procedure. Rather quickly, they figured out that if they paid them by the sackful, it made a vast difference in the rate at which the potatoes were picked off the field.

A potato grader was set up in the field, a huge machine that the potatoes were fed into on one end; it then cleaned them and the small ones fell through. The potatoes still needed to be sorted and graded by hand. Some of them were sold right there, straight out of the ground in the one hundred pound sacks. The majority were loaded onto a railroad car to be shipped.

Those that weren't sold right away had to be hauled to the massive root cellar that Fred Kozuki and his crew of three or four men were building. Although it did not have a roof yet, the potatoes were hauled in anyway, and the roof was finished before the potatoes were all in.

Willie Hannah operated the agency for marketing the potatoes, and kept part of the profit as commission. They hauled the potatoes by truck, using Mike's three quarter ton truck, and another truck owned by Sid Pigeon.

The cellar filled up with about one hundred and fifty tons, around 300,000 pounds – literally a mountain of spuds. The price was good ($1.00 a sack), and all the potatoes were sold. Enough potatoes were kept in the cellar to use for seed the following spring.

If Mike thought he was going to get a rest from potatoes that winter, he was mistaken. They had to be constantly checked for spoilage, as one hidden rotting potato would wreck all of the potatoes that surrounded it. The spuds were moved from one bin into another, removing any rotten ones. They had special big-tined forks to scoop out potatoes and move them around. The bins were made so that one board could be taken out from the bottom, allowing the potatoes to fall out when they needed more to check.

This was a full-time task that carried on all winter. Once again, Mike was anxious to haul the seed potatoes out of the cellar and into the ground in the spring. So far he had not had a break from the sight and smell and the thought of potatoes.

The following year they hired six potato cutters from the Sugarcane Reserve – Henry Wycotte and his wife, James Louie and his wife, Rosie Mouse, and Mrs. Chow Lo Dick. They were planting certified seed this year, as it was worth more money, so extra care had to be taken in planting. If one potato would make four sprouts, it would be cut only partway through, so that it would still stay together. They used the potato planter with the rotating wheel table, and with these certain potatoes, they would break them apart, but skip a hole in the disk. This way there was a space around these plants when they grew, and you could tell that these were the good ones.

They were monitored carefully. If one plant showed a disease (Giant Hill, Witches Broom, ring rot, etc.), all the potatoes from that plant and the gap around it, would be pulled, put in a bag, hauled off the field and burned. They harvested about ten acres of certified seed, and about forty acres of commercial potatoes in the fall. Again, they all sold. The huge root cellar filled to capacity, then steadily emptied out again.

Large orders were sold at a cheap price to private buyers. The cull potatoes (small or knobby or scabby) were fed to the cattle in the winter. Occasionally the cattle would choke on the potatoes. When they saw a cow gagging in this manner, they would take hold of the lump in their throat and work it either down or up to save the cow from choking. Sometimes they weren't successful.

The dam at Felker Lake was holding more water this spring, and needed rebuilding. Dave Pierce and Ken Isnardy, Ray Pigeon, and Wilfred Pinchbeck did most of this work. They replaced the little wooden box with a pipe, then had to pull a dirt mover with a little Ford Ferguson tractor to cover it.

The potato business was so far quite successful, despite the extra time and work. In 1952, the following spring, they decided to go all out and put in *ninety* acres of potato seed. This meant much preparation of the land as it was hayland, and the previous fields that had grown potatoes had to be put back into hayfields again. Using the same fields any longer boosted your chances of producing scabby potatoes.

The new fields were full of rocks, not only on top, but under the soil as well. A major rockpicking effort had to be organized first – loads and loads of rocks were piled onto stoneboats and removed from the fields. The larger rocks, for the most part buried beneath the soil, had to be blown with dynamite. Mike soon found that this did not agree with him at all. Breathing the fumes from the dynamite affected him. After a day of dynamiting, he was so nauseated he couldn't eat supper at night. He would go to bed, feel better the next morning, then the whole procedure would start over again.

Now these new acres of potatoes were close to the hayfields that had a lot of weeds growing in them. Although they had basically the same crew as before, they could not keep up with the weeds. Seeing how behind they were getting, Mike went to see Doc Avery and Sid Pigeon.

"The potatoes are full of weeds, they're growing

faster than we can pull them!" he told them, barely hiding his frustration.

"Get more help then, however many it takes,' they claimed, "weeds in the potatoes will make a poor crop!"

Mike hurried to the Sugarcane Reserve and hired ten more people to weed. After a few days, it was apparent they were not going to get caught up, even with these extra weeders. Mike drove back to Sugarcane Reserve and hired another eleven people. There were now around twenty-five people, including himself, weeding what seemed like endless rows in the potato fields. They camped right there by the fields in tents, cooking for themselves, and stayed for three weeks.

Finally the crop looked presentable again. Then it took two trips back to Sugarcane Reserve just to haul all the weeders' tents and camping gear back.

All this time they were tending to the potato problem, the ranch work was suffering. The haying had to be done, and the irrigating, added to the extra watering that the new potato fields needed.

Then harvest-time hit.

"I haven't slept for six weeks!" Mike lamented, as he heaved yet another cumbersome sack of potatoes into the back of the truck. All the natives had been hired back to pick potatoes. Mike would take Amedee out to the field as early in the morning as they could see. Then he would haul potatoes until ten or eleven o'clock at night, sometimes they didn't quit until one o'clock in the morning.

Finally the digging was finished; they were disappointed to discover there were a large quantity of culls (knobby ones). A lot of these went to the local dairy for cow feed. Not only that, but they had sold so many seed potatoes that everybody was now growing their own potatoes, and not many were buying. It was hard to find buyers for the main crop.

The only thing to do was to feed them to the cattle, and this meant another time-consuming process of cooking them. They were feeding about one hundred and sixty head of Lees cattle, and they cooked up about a ton of potatoes for them. He managed to sell a good bunch to Lionel Singlehurst for his dairy cows for $10.00 a truckload.

The cellar was now filled to capacity with potatoes, and it was not emptying out as in the former years. There were tons that had not sold, and Mike could smell rotten ones but could not get to them as there were simply too many to move around. He tried to give them away just to get them out of the cellar. There were potatoes in the field, in the cellar, in the trucks, and in Mike's dreams, when he did get a chance to sleep. He could smell them everywhere. When the potatoes at the bottom started rotting and they couldn't get to them, the smell was evident from the main road.

Finally Mike had had enough. He hired three people with a truck for about a week to haul the potatoes out of the cellar and dump them into a gully and the Fraser River just to get rid of them.

That was the end of the A&P potato production days.

The A& P Ranch sold to Pudge Moon, who asked Mike to stay on, but Mike was so afraid of seeing another potato, that he was ready to move on. He had given the potatoes a good part of his energy, his attention and his life over the past few years – heck, he even rode in a huge potato sack in the Williams Lake Stampede parade, enduring much jesting and "spud" jokes.

Mike retired from the potato business, and left his brother Kenny in charge.

The huge root cellar was eventually used by the Moon family for grain storage. One day Rex Moon and Bert Johnson were grinding grain in the cellar. They had a tractor running, with a belt hooked to a grinder at the back. At one point Rex yelled to Bert, who was working at the far end of the belt. Getting no response, he headed to where Bert had been, and found him lying on the ground. Suddenly, he found that he could barely stand up either. Realizing they must be the victims of fumes, he managed to shut the tractor off. Then, stumbling and partially-fainting, he managed to drag Bert and himself outside to the fresh air. They had had a close call with carbon dioxide poisoning from the diesel fumes of the tractor.

Potato King

Luckily, except for some excruciating headaches, they were none the worse for wear.

*Threshing crew at Staffords*

*The dam at Staffords*

*Potato King*

# Getting Modern

## Chapter 13

The telephone was coming in to Dog Creek – a long-awaited event that excited the entire neighbour-hood. Everyone anxiously awaited their turn to get hooked up to the magic invention that would make communication so much faster and easier.

Mike didn't get too excited, the telephone didn't make much difference to his life. He still spent most of his time either outdoors on a trail, or at various cow camps and cabins where no telephone lines would be strung, in any event.

As the talking lines crept further and further into the outlying areas around Williams Lake, Mike's parents James and Evelyn, kept Mike informed of the advantages of having the apparatus in their home.

One day a local cowboy in the Dog Creek area, Pete Barker, was repairing a line between Dog Creek and Pigeon's ranch. For the most part, trees were used as poles to hold the wire, and this particular line had been knocked down and broken by a falling branch. Partway up a tree, he had tied the end of a coil of loose wire around his waist, to give himself two free hands to splice with. The other end of the coil spiralled loosely to the ground.

Down the narrow road came local Jimmy Syme, bumping along in his panel truck. He waved when he saw Pete perched partway up the tree. As the truck passed by, the bumper on the back of the panel truck hooked the loop of wire that was strung from Pete's waist to the ground. With a sudden jerk, Pete was propelled down from the tree and began a bouncing running dance in a cloud of dust behind the panel truck. Unable to stay on his feet, he tumbled to the ground, to be dragged on his belly, hanging on to the wire with both hands, yelling at the top of his lungs for Jimmy to stop.

Jimmy Syme continued on his drive, the roaring of the engine and the rocky road made him oblivious to the shrieking cargo he was dragging. He finally thought he heard a strange noise and bumped to a stop. He was amazed to hear swearing and cursing coming from the rear of his truck. Climbing down from his truck, he headed towards the racket and stared dumbfounded at the dirty tattered raving spectacle clambering to his feet, his clothing ripped and torn and, for the most part, not even there anymore. Jimmy remarked afterwards that "there wasn't much more than his collar left."

Vehicles, the horseless wagons, were a fascinating new item. Many people who had the means to buy one, did so, then afterwards longed for their horses when they realized this new machine got stuck on the muddy roads, could not traverse creeks, ran out of fuel, and sometimes just sat and spewed forth hot angry steam from under its hood, for no particular reason at all.

Mike watched these new advances with interest, but was not anxious to give up his reliable horses in the face of the many stories he heard relating to the new self-propelled wheeled vehicles. They were not always built to suit everyone. Hank Krynen knew a fellow in Holland who was seven feet tall. His new vehicle, a Prefect, could not accommodate his height, so he cut a hole in the top for his head to fit through. He became a regular sight, driving around town with his head sticking out the top of his car.

The roads were not advancing or improving as quickly as the novelty vehicles. Some found their work load actually made much more difficult – there were many accounts of farmers and ranchers who had experiences that resulted in much lost time and effort. He heard about Herb Chesley, who lived on the west side of the Fraser River between Williams Lake and Quesnel. On one particularly wet day, he loaded up a whole truckful of lumber and proceeded up the road to do a delivery. His truck mired down in the mud, and he was forced to unload all the lumber by hand to lighten the truck enough so they could pry it out of the mudhole. Then of course, the lumber all had to be reloaded by hand back into the truck.

A 5-ton International truck from the Circle S tipped over on the muddy soft road at Cape Horn near Alkali. It was filled with sacked grain pellets, which all spilled

Getting Modern

off the truck and subsequently had to be loaded back on again afterwards.

Mike heard these accounts, and decided to stick with his trusty four-footed vehicles.

The new machines did not stop to the "WHOA" command, as some unwary drivers found out. Angus Grewar, an acquaintance of Mike's and a fine Scottish laddie from the Mission area, just south of WIlliams Lake, later moved to Cochrane, Alberta. One frigid winter evening, the coldest night of the winter, his wife Paula drove to the local Red Rooster store, and Angus jumped in to keep her company. She parked in front of the store only to discover that the hand-brake had frozen and she would have to shut the engine off while she did her shopping, leaving the car in gear so that it wouldn't roll.

Angus waited patiently in the passenger's seat, blowing on his hands and trying to keep warm. He finally decided the heater would be on if the vehicle was running, and reached over and turned the key on. Before he could get his lanky 6'3" frame behind the steering wheel to do anything about it, the vehicle drove right through the front wall and plate glass window of the Red Rooster Store.

Paula was standing at the checkout counter when she heard a strange booming sound and then watched in utter stunned amazement as her car, with Angus still sitting in the passenger's seat, bulldozed its way through the broken wall, past the checkout, and came to rest in the collapsing tinned goods section.

Angus was a colorful character. He and Paula worked at St. Joseph's Mission in the Sugarcane area, looking after the cows and calves. Angus took great pride in his Scottish heritage, and had a penchant for wearing his native kilt wherever he went.

Angus developed a problem after an episode of dehorning one spring. The animals were run into a chute, and their heads held securely while one cowboy "snipped" off the horns with a heavy metal clipper-type instrument. To stop the shorn-off stubs from bleeding excessively, the cowboys applied a white powder to the area.

*Getting Modern*

Angus began to experience some discomfort with his private parts, and at the end of the day was horrified to discover that his penis was enlarged, red and swollen. He kept quiet about it, hoping that it would go away. It didn't.

After more silent suffering and realizing that soon Paula would be questioning as to why he was walking so strangely – as though he were riding a horse, when he actually wasn't - he confided his problem to her. She promptly called the doctor and Angus was forced to reveal his painful situation once again.

"In over thirty years of practice, I've never seen anything like this!" the perplexed doctor remarked, as he paced back and forth, pulling at his chin, surveying Angus' distended and discomforting parts.

Finally, he pulled a chair into the center of the examining room. "Here, why don't you climb up on this chair, and jump down as hard as you can. Maybe it will fall off, and you won't have to worry about it anymore!"

Then, more seriously, he queried as to the activities Angus had been involved in before it all started – had he been in contact with any strange substances, or poisons, etc.?

Angus scratched his head and thought back to that day, when it had been his job to apply the Caustic white powder to the cut horn bases. They concluded that this must have been the cause of his dilemma.

In time, Angus healed up with the assistance of some very expensive ointment. He suffered the added injury of facing his mother-in-law at the breakfast table every morning, as she inquired "And 'ow are your private parts this mornin' Angus?"

One cold and blustery March evening, they had attended the local Scottish supper to celebrate Robert Burn's Day in Williams Lake. Although there had been thawing, it had frozen again, and on the way home their vehicle couldn't make it up the icy incline of the Mission Road. Paula stayed behind the wheel to steer, and Angus slid in his dress shoes around to the back to push.

Following behind them was another vehicle. A group of local natives were taking advantage of the slow progress that Angus was making, and thoroughly

*Getting Modern*

enjoying the spectacle he created. With his long stork-like legs, and stockings up to his knobby knees, and his kilt whipping up around his ears in the wind, he braved the elements to keep his shoulder to the back bumper.

Angus even wore his kilt when he went to war. His regiment, under the U.N. flag, was stationed on a long route march on the North African Desert. A Scottish Battalion wasn't complete without a piper – they marched mile after stifling-hot mile across the unforgiving desert to the bagpiper's windy lament. The heat was unbearable, and Angus watched as buzzards circled slowly and hopefully overhead, no doubt expecting some unlucky soldier to collapse and drop to the ground with heat prostration.

Although their swinging kilts allowed air to circulate from the bottom – Scotsmen do not wear underwear beneath their kilts – the woollen waistbands and top parts of the kilts soon became sweat-soaked and uncomfortable. At one point, their battalion leader called a halt and ordered all his troops to remove their kilts.

Approximately one thousand soldiers removed their kilts and stood bare-butted, as they waited for the order to turn them inside out and re-dress, allowing them a uniform change of sorts – at least a drier waistband for awhile.

Another new addition to the Cariboo area was the Rudy Johnson Bridge across the mighty Fraser River. This was the brainchild of an enterprising man by the name of Rudy Johnson. He owned the Buckskin Ranch, located on the west side of the Fraser River. A trip to Williams Lake meant a long detour around to the Soda Creek Ferry, or alternatively all the way around to the Sheep Creek Bridge.

When his wife was pregnant with twins, he was understandably a mite nervous that he wouldn't be able to make the trip to town quickly enough when the time came. He joked that he was going to put her into a pair of his bib overalls and sew the bottoms of the legs shut, just as a precaution.

Rudy approached officials from the government Transport and Highways departments, to seek their assistance to install a bridge. They scoffed at the idea.

Getting Modern

"The chasm is four hundred feet deep at that point – you would never get pilings to stay" or "The cost would be too great". No one took him seriously.

Rudy was a far-sighted man, and not one to be easily deterred from an idea he felt would work. He bought a used bridge for $40,000 from Alaska, a steel and wood structure that was three hundred feet long. With the help of a few private business partners, the bridge was transported by rail and truck to the site on the Fraser River directly below his ranch. He hired an engineer to help with the construction plans, but basically had it all figured in his head how it would work.

Work began immediately, and soon the only privately owned toll bridge across a major river in Western Canada stretched proudly from one side of the river to the other, cutting almost forty miles from his travel distance every time he went to Williams Lake. He eventually sold it to the government, and it is still in full use today.

It was a personal triumph against overwhelming odds for a "man with a vision".

The new bridge connected the two sides of the river and made life much handier for many people west of the Fraser River. Medical situations were not so crucial; people and animals' lives were saved, as the doctors and veterinarians could be called out to emergency situations and be there in a reasonable amount of time. This saved much wear and tear and extra stress for already-injured individuals and animals.

Mike Isnardy had reason to call upon the services of just such a mobile veterinarian one day.

This was not only a hard life, filled with hard work for these cowboys and ranchers. It was tough on animals. In the spring, as the sullen winter thawed and made way for calving time, Mike rode up to check on the Lees cattle that had been moved up the river in the early spring to catch the first spring green grass.

He noticed a newborn calf, and rode up to it to make sure all was well, his dog following close behind. The mother cow, a long-horned Hereford, took exception to the border collie, and came charging. Her horn hooked the horse Grey Eagle in the front of his chest, piercing

Getting Modern

through the skin, and lifting him right off the ground.

Mike urged the squealing horse away as fast as possible and, when there was a safe distance between them and the mad mother, he got off to survey the damage. Grey Eagle stood, feet apart and head down, wheezing; with every breath he took, some frothy material came out from the hole the horn had left.

When Mike realized the severity of the gash, he set off immediately for home, walking, leading Grey Eagle, keeping his exertion at as low a level as possible. Talking softly all the way, he coaxed the faltering horse to keep heading towards home.

It was over an hour before he was able to phone veterinarian Dr. Woods, and relay to him what had happened.

Dr. Woods drove out to take a look at the injured horse. He shook his head when he saw the deep gash in Grey Eagle's chest. "It's a punctured windpipe - I can't do anything to help him. Just make sure the wound stays clean and keep the horse as quiet as possible, see if it heals up."

Mike followed these instructions faithfully, keeping Grey Eagle penned in close vicinity so that he could make sure the wound stayed clean without infection, and no other animals were around to bother him. Grey Eagle improved steadily, and after six weeks it was hard to tell that he had suffered such a trauma.

This horse Grey Eagle went from one disaster to another.

A cowboy borrowed Grey Eagle to check the cattle. As there had been warm balmy weather, he had been fit with horseshoes for the rocky terrain. An unexpected bout of winter turned the previously thawed areas to ice, and Grey Eagle was having a hard time keeping his footing with the slippery metal horseshoes sliding around on the ice.

The concerned rider got off the horse and led him, thinking that would help. Snow by this time had balled up in the shoes, and the horse could not get its footing. Grey Eagle started to slip on a side hill, was powerless to stop his descent, the slippery horseshoes pawing uselessly at the icy slope. The fearful cowboy finally

Getting Modern

had to let go of the reins and could only watch helplessly as Grey Eagle went sliding over a seventy-five-foot drop. A sickening thud ended his descent far below.

He scrambled down the bank to where Grey Eagle lay perfectly still. The horse was dead, and the saddle, belonging to Doc Avery, was wrecked. The unhappy cowboy had to walk back to the ranch with the bad news.

The next day he and Amedee went back and lowered themselves over the cliff with ropes to retrieve the saddle. The rigging was all stretched out of shape, as the horse had bloated up overnight. They bundled up the wreckage and took it to Tony's Leather Goods, owned by Polish shoemaker Tony Borkowski, who had come from Manitoba and learned the rudiments of shoemaking and working with leather from his father. Also working there was Tommy Denny, a leather craftsman who would later own and operate a family saddlery shop well-known to all as Cariboo Saddlery. They took over the difficult task of transforming the pile of broken pieces back into a saddle. It came out looking as good as new. Mike wished they could have done the same for Grey Eagle. He had been a good horse, and it was a while before Mike found a suitable replacement for his strength and speed.

The deer were causing considerable damage and giving the ranchers headaches. Their numbers seemed to increase, rather than decrease, even though they shot as many as they could. The sheer numbers of these deer meant the loss of much valuable hay, especially the valuable second crop of alfalfa. They would climb on top of the hay stacks and tramp it solid with their sharp hooves. It would then freeze that way, and be difficult to fork out in the winter months. They were a pest, and at the top of the ranchers list to be eliminated.

It didn't seem to matter how many they shot – the deer flourished and continued to harass the ranchers with their haying enterprises. Les Joeman was the local game warden, and the ranchers kept a watchful eye out for him, as he took his job seriously and was rigid in carrying out his duties.

Getting Modern

# Rattlesnake Medicine

## Chapter 14

It was the mid 1950's, and change was creeping in on the ranching enterprises. As sure as a tide encroaching further and steadily further onto a shore, it was constant, inevitable and unstoppable. Telephones and vehicles and machinery were commonplace; the cattle drives were quickly becoming a thing of the past, horses were turned out to become wild and hunted. Railway cars became a faster and more efficient mode to ship cattle.

Some ranchers accompanied their cattle on their railroad rides to market.

Mike Isnardy headed to Vancouver by rail with twenty-five head of cattle. This was an adventurous occasion for him, new territory, certainly a different scene from the bush trails and solitary cabin life he had come to know. His stomping grounds were surrounded by large ranching outfits – The Alkali Lake Ranch, the Circle S at Dog Creek, and the massive more remote Gang Ranch across the Fraser River. Occasionally the people on these outfits got together, but the work was constant and never-relenting, and the many hours needed to travel to and from these outfits were precious work hours lost.

Young men constantly came from faraway places, with dreams of the romantic cowboy life in their heads. They would generally be on foot, and would drift from outfit to outfit seeking the best wages, benefits, and the most tolerant managers.

One such young energetic man was Daniel Praud. He came from the southern Alberta area near Calgary, and thumbed and scraped his way to the city of Kamloops, constantly on the lookout for a way to maneuver himself to the outer rural areas where the large ranches would hopefully hire a greenhorn. These young hopefuls would take any kind of travel accommodations and often found themselves riding in the rail cars with the cattle. This was of course a ride that, although lacking somewhat in comfort, didn't cost them anything, and the railroad engineers and conductors tended to turn a blind eye to their fareless travel. It was a help to them, as these fellows could stop the cattle from bunching up, and get an animal up on its feet when it was in danger of being trampled by the others. These free rides were many times cold, miserable, and stinky – the stowaways would huddle against the cattle for warmth.

Daniel Praud successfully landed up on the Gang Ranch, and his determination to get past the greenhorn choreboy stage soon made him an accepted part of the crew. He would do anything he was told, and spent much of his early time there helping the cook out with all the cookhouse and garden duties. This diminutive Chinese cook was well-known in the area for his medicinal inclinations. He had everyone on the lookout for rattlesnakes, as these were a vital part of his medicine. The snakes were usually caught in the irrigation ditches, and were brought to the Chinaman. The first thing he would do was to sew the rattlesnake's mouth shut with some strong string. He could then keep the snakes without feeding them, until their bodies were emptied of impurities. Then they were killed, stuffed into a jar and covered with gin. The longer this unsavory concoction sat, the more potent it became, and any-one suffering from rheumatism got a dose of the Chinaman's snake medicine.

The Gang Ranch in the 1950's was a going concern – an historic million-acre ranch that evolved from the Harper brothers, Thadeus and Jerome, who rustled herds of cattle up from the U.S. to the seemingly unending grasslands there, and eventually laid claim to the vast and expansive Gang Ranch area. It acquired the name Gang Ranch from the horsedrawn land-breaking ploughing implement called the "gang plough".

Numerous Chinese people who had drifted through the area following the building of the railway, wound up on the Gang Ranch, their well-tended vegetable gardens and goldpanning operations dotted the banks of the Fraser River. They moved water from one area to another, sometimes miles and miles, in overhead "ditches" – wooden flumes, downhill chutes, built laboriously on top of periodic wooden supports, all done by hand. The flumes, although broken and rotted in places, still stand as ghostly monuments to these industrious people throughout the Cariboo region. Numerous Chinese utensils, such as deep round hand-carved wooden spoons, metal hand-shaped soup ladles, and bowls, are still found along the Fraser River. What were mere necessities to them are now valuable artifacts to us.

Also on the Ranch, indigenous as the very soil beneath their mocassined feet, were the native Indians who inhabited the many valleys and areas of the mighty Gang. Although they didn't hold paper title to these lands, it was their birthplace, and their life-time homes, they spent their lives working on the Ranch. There were the Wycott ancestors, who raised longhorn cattle on the lush green lower banks of Churn Creek, an area later called Wycott Flats, and the Rosettes.

The native Rosette family was a pillar of lifelong knowledge of this territory and its cowboying and cattle, haying and irrigation, and fencing and farming operations. Old Jimmy Rosette (Jiggs) blazed all the trails in the back country that led through forests, valleys and creeks, connecting thirteen different cow camps, to the very back of the Ranch property in the high alpine country of the coastal mountains. The Rosette family grew large and far-reaching, and were also integral building blocks on Alkali Lake Ranch, and the Dog Creek and Canoe Creek areas.

The natives claimed there was a longtime curse that obsessed the Gang Ranch, the source possibly being the deaths of an entire native hunting band of twenty who were all found dead around their campfire in remote Graveyard Valley. It seemed to follow, with eerie coincidence, that every owner of the Gang Ranch from that time even up to the present day, met with some manner of disaster and calamity. The sad culmination of this seeming curse is that today the people who loved the Ranch, formed the foundation of the present Ranch, lived their lives working and respecting her, have all been forced to leave. Old Jimmy Rosette suffered the disrespect of having the particular little home he had been born in, and lived in all his life, simply gone when he went there one day. He died shortly thereafter, still speaking of the shock of having his home disappear.

The sprawling old matriarch Gang Ranch, through a shameful labyrinth of legal and banking skullduggery (outlined in my book called Gang Ranch the Real Story) has been placed by the Canadian Imperial Bank of Commerce into the hands of foreign owner Saudi Arabian Ibrahim Afandi. Afandi first bought shares in the ranch from the CIBC in 1984, before the Alsager family could even appeal a very questionable decision made by a position-driven Judge that the CIBC should own the Gang Ranch.

By 1988, Afandi had bought out all the other shareholders, to become owner of this massive prime acreage, at that time approximately one-sixth of the land mass of British Columbia.

Despite all these murky moves by greedy and politically-driven sheisters, the Gang Ranch was and still remains unmatched as a massive beautiful spread. Its sheer size and range of topography makes it a one-of-a-kind empire.

You can travel from the one end that is bordering Dog Creek and the Fraser River, which is semi-arid, open fields, and cactus-strewn, all the way to the back end high up in the alpine coastal mountain peaks, eighty five miles as the crow flies. Clear glacial waters of Lorna Lake form the headwaters, fingering out into meandering creeks in all directions, to eventually wind up as the main water feed for the Ranch. If you travelled from the main Ranch yard to the headwaters, you would pass through four seasons, and the most spectacular scenery anywhere.

Another of Mike Isnardy's large cattle spread

neighbours was the historic Alkali Lake Ranch. Located nearer to Springhouse and Williams Lake than the Gang Ranch and Dog Creek, it started out as a hundred and sixty acre preemption property purchased for five dollars by Herman Bowe, a miner from Barkerville.

Starting a lineage of tough horsemen and rodeo riders, in 1863 he drove five hundred head of durable Texas longhorn cattle up from Oregon to establish the makings of a cattle ranch. It grew to two thousand acres, and a public stopping house run by Henry Bowe. In addition to the duties of running such a large spread, they provided lodging and accommodations for travellers – good homecooked meals, a livery stable, and even a bar with wines, liquors and cigars. In 1948 the River Ranch part of this territory was sold to Mario Reideman.

Henry's son Alfred Bowe became a cowboy on the Alkali Lake Ranch. Alfred was a master hand with horses. At the age of twelve, he was driving four and six horse teams on heavy-laden freight wagons, from Ashcroft and back and as far out as Bechers House at Riske Creek. All freight from Ashcroft going to Canoe Creek, Empire Valley, Gang Ranch, Dog Creek, and Alkali area, travelled on this road. The trails were perilous, muddy and rutted much of the time. He sometimes would make this arduous journey three times in a span of ten days.

An important and valuable freight he hauled were cases and cases of liquor. On one particular stormy miserable trip, his freight became bogged down and he was forced to leave it. It was mostly cases of liquor, and he was certain that by the next day, someone would have been deliriously happy about finding all that liquor. When he returned the next day, he was surprised to find it all just where he had left it. Alfred became somewhat famous for his wild habit of crossing the dangerous Fraser River with horses, supplies, and cattle herds. He would often ride his white stallion into the swift-moving current, slide off and hang onto his tail to cross the river.

Hauling freight and other necessities was a much-needed service in those days. Another local ranching worker and cowboy was Lenny DeRose, who had a sleigh with wheels and hauled water to the hookers at Barkerville. Chow Lee, from his spread way up by the Marguerite Ferry on the west side of the river, used to haul tons upon tons of produce and meat to Williams Lake on a weekly basis – potatoes, carrots, onions, turnips, pigs, chickens and beef. The heavy freight wagons had to be kept well-maintained, as the worst thing that could happen would be to have to unload four tons of potatoes to be able to change a wheel.

The Alkali Lake Ranch flourished through the years to become one of the most successful and well-respected operations in the area, up to the present-day ownership of Doug and Marie Mervin. Many fine families have descended from the original owners, and cowboys, farmers, rodeo riders, have played there, worked there, left and returned. Cattle, horses, haying, the stopping-over house and livery stable, were all integral steps in the success of this ranch.

They even had hunters and adventurers coming by to sample the bountiful wildlife in the area, especially in the area above Moose Meadows in the Lac La Hache area. Cecilia Dick, later to become wife to Lenny Derose, helped her family in the guiding business, and used to watch in wonder as some American hunters from Tacoma Washington brought pillows out of their luggage and tied them on to their saddles before they got on to ride.

Henry (Hank) Krynen was a long-time farm manager on the Alkali Lake Ranch. Originally from Holland, he and his English wife, Julie, fit into the mould of ranching life and its many and varied experiences. They had a son, Andrew, and a daughter, Joanne, who attended the predominantly native school at Alkali Lake. Julie kept up her nursing profession by driving to Williams Lake to work at the Cariboo Memorial Hospital. The roads were mere rutted trails in those days before highway maintenance was invented.

On one particular journey in to work on a blizzardy New Year's Day, Julie found herself at the mercy of the elements, as the heavy wet snow completely obliterated any clue as to where the road even was.

"Call in to work in an hour or so to make sure I get there," she called out to Hank, as she headed out the door into whiteout conditions. Her Toyota Hatchback plodded along bravely, not a single other vehicle was in sight. Julie carried on as it became more and more difficult to tell which was road or ditch. Soon she realized she had no idea where the road was. As it was senseless to think of turning around, she kept on going until the car ground to a halt, hopelessly stuck.

She climbed out of the car and promptly fell over in deep snow. Floundering around, she found what appeared to be a rail underneath her car, and realized that it was parked smack on top of the rustle fence that bordered the Dog Creek Road.

For the next five hours, she walked, plowing through snow well over her knees, to various ranches and yards. She couldn't find anyone home, as most of the ranchers were out feeding their hungry animals in the storm. Deflated, and fearing she would freeze if she didn't get to the shelter of her vehicle, she trudged back to the Toyota accompanied by the steady humming of the overhead telephone and hydro wires over the hushed countryside. She thought that surely by now Hank would have come looking for her.

She waited and waited, all the while cursing Hank as she had figured out by now that he must have forgotten to phone the hospital to check that she arrived there.

Finally in the afternoon the Johnsons, a neighbouring couple, happened along. After much maneuvering and digging, her car was back on the road, pointed towards home.

As she headed back towards Alkali, she came upon a figure furiously shovelling his truck out of a snowdrift. There was something very familiar about this person, and with a laugh, she realized it was Hank. Still seething from her long wait in the frigid cold, she sailed right on by him with a gay wave of her hand.

Many horsemen and cowboys worked in the area, and formed a tightfitting hardworking lifelong relationship of similar likes and lives. Longtime cowboy and cattle buyer Red Allison was in the Dog Creek area until 1957; Eric Reay worked at Dog Creek, and was there when the first vehicles started traveling the treacherous switchbacks. The locals were used to horseback, this was fairly terrifying at times for them. After one particular fast trip in a motor vehicle around the switchbacks headed towards the Gang Ranch from Dog Creek, Eric asked Tommy Harry, a native of Dog Creek, how he had enjoyed the ride. Tommy caught his breath and answered, "Purty scairt – my ass was so tight, I could-a cut a rope with it!"

Vehicles were an exciting invention, but did have their shortcomings. Ray Pigeon had just built a brand new pole gate, and he was very proud of it. It had taken him a full week's work of cutting the logs, peeling them and laboriously shaping them to a perfection fit. Finally, there it hung in all its elegance.

Along came Hank Krynen in his Jeep Stationwagon, giving Ray's son, Jimmy, a ride home. Jimmy was animately relaying to Hank all the merits of the new gate. As they approached it, Hank whistled in admiration at the still-bright peeled logs. He rolled up to it and stepped on the brakes to stop. Nothing happened.

There were no brakes and the station wagon went crashing right through the shiny peeled logs of the new gate, carrying on down the road, wearing the gate wrapped around it just like a picture frame.

Music and dancing were events everyone looked forward to, and a local dance brought people from far away, and was a chance for the cowboys and ranch workers to get together and let off some steam. These were the times they got to visit with neighbouring people from out of the area where distance and poor roads made getting together difficult and rare.

The wooden structure army barracks at the Dog Creek Airport field had a dance hall, and the dances they held there were formal affairs. Stiff-necked dignitaries in fancy suits and fancy-attired ladies were invited. Indians were not allowed – perhaps because at that time they were not permitted in establishments that served liquor.

The natives were the foundation of the surrounding communities, important and longstanding families who were an integral part of all local activities, business and goings-on. Hank Krynen and Bill Twan decided to test the rules of this particular formal dance.

They dressed up as Indians – Bill as a native lady, with long braids and a burlap sack skirt and a cloak-like shawl. Hank was the brave, with a cloth hat, native knitted Siwash sweater, and a brightly colored kerchief. Someone darkened his face with brown paint. Bill carried an Indian baby basket. They had a little brown jug with them, full of tea supplied by Bill's wife, Jock Twan. In all appearances, it looked like a jug of wine.

They made their way in to the crowded dance hall, past all the fancy dresses and suits, right to the middle of the dance floor. There they sat down, folded their legs in, and proceeded to pass the jug back and forth to each other.

Very quickly the dance floor vacated, the dancers moved to the edges, stared in amazement, whispered and pointed. The music ground to a halt, and silence prevailed as the two Indians, now the centre of attention, continued peacefully guzzling their tea.

They stayed for the rest of the night, and certainly got their point across.

The Twan family was an integral part of the history of the Alkali Lake Ranch. Hank Krynen laughingly prodded Mrs. Jock Twan with the cattle prod once. (A cattle prod is actually a stick-like prod that gives an electric shock to the animal to get it moving). Mrs. Twan bided her time to repay him, waiting cagily until he no longer expected retaliation.

One Sunday, a peaceful frozen morning of –36 degrees, she grabbed her opportunity. Hank was delighted to find the sweathouse unoccupied, and proceeded to light up a huge fire to produce lots of steam. On previous visits to the sweathouse, Jimmy Beaulieu and Moise Robbins had blocked the entry-way for Hank to leave the steamy hot and cramped area – he almost had to claw his way out of the canvas at the back to get some fresh air.

On that frigid morning, with no-one around, Hank poured water over the sizzling rocks until the small tent was filled with steaming vapor. Dropping his clothes outside, he ducked inside and closed the canvas flap behind him.

You can't stay in a sweathouse for very long, and soon he ventured out to pick up his clothes.

They were gone. Then Hank saw an apparition coming towards him. He recognized Jock Twan's big fur coat and scarf, and recalled her threats when he had zapped her with the stock prod. Outstretched in front, this person held the stock prod and headed with great determination straight for Hank and his naked-ness. Clothes or no, away ran Hank, stark naked in the –36 weather. He took refuge racing through the cover of a bush where the frozen willows were merciless on his bare hide. Hot on his trail was the fur coat apparition, who was actually Bill Twan dressed in his wife's clothing, menacing the stock prod.

Hank's natural good nature made him a target for pranksters and fun-making – everyone knew he would laugh about it afterwards.

Gang Ranch Headquarters

Cattle being driven over old Gang Ranch Bridge

Earl Cahill photo

Dan Proud at the Gang Ranch, with
rattlesnake for chinese cooks medicine

Dan Proud photo

Hank Krynen and Bill Twan, Dog Creek Airport Party 1958
Al Becker photo, courtesy of Robert Becker

# Haying & Ranching & Sawmilling

## Chapter 15

**M**ike was working at Pinchbeck's. They sold the cows and bought a saw mill from Herb Auld at 100 Mile House. This mill was set up at Bill Stafford's at Springhouse. Amedee, Richie and Mike threw themselves into the sawmill operation.

In May of 1954 Amedee and Mike partnered up with Pete Rasmussen. Amedee went to the ranch to help Pete, while Mike and Richie stayed with the mill until the haying season. In July Mike moved to the ranch to help Amedee and Pete with the haying.

Pete sold twenty some head of dry cows in August, shipping them to Vancouver at Tom Baird's sale. Mike went once again to Vancouver with the cattle on the train. He left Williams Lake one night, travelled through Lillooet, Seton Lake, and finally got to Squamish. Then it was a trip by boat to Vancouver. He thought they were never going to get there. He was anxious to get back to work, as Pete was not well. He returned by bus, which was much faster.

Shortly after the haying season, Pete died, leaving the ranch to Mike and Amedee. Ken took the mill over.

Amedee and Mike rented Peavine Pasture near de Sous Rd.from their Auntie Hortence and Charlie Tressiera and had lots of hay left over. They sold the steers and eighteen head of the older cows. Mike and Mel Mayfield did a cattle drive to Vancouver in November.That fall they had to buy enough cows to keep the range going. Pudge Moon sold them fifty-nine head, and later they bought thirty head from Ralph Inscho, along with two bulls. Before they knew it, their herd grew to four hundred head. Louis Dan fed them in the meadows until his wife died. Then other arrangements had to be made.

Mike went around the community and bought

haystacks from those who cut and stacked it on the meadows. He wanted to ensure he had an adequate supply for the winter months ahead. He would measure the stacks as they stood in the meadows and pay the owners of the stacks accordingly.

Tommy Harry and Mitchell Dick offered to sell Mike a haystack they had piled between some stacking poles in Shorty's Meadow. Mike walked around the stack as he always did, measuring and calculating, and paid them for the tonnage he had come up with.

All went well until winter came, and the time arrived for Mike to feed this hay to his cattle. He plunged his fork in to throw hay off, but the fork hit something hard. Puzzled, he tried another spot, and another and another. Every place he attempted to shove the fork into resulted in hitting something very solid. He finally climbed on top of the stack and proceeded to throw hay off.

There were mammoth boulders everywhere in this area, and Tommy and Mitchell had selected a huge boulder the size of a haystack, and very cleverly concealed it on all sides with as much hay as it took to hide what it actually was.

Mike grimaced as he realized that at this very moment they were no doubt sitting by their fires, consumed with laughter, as they knew he was headed up there to do the feeding.

This wasn't the only time a purchased haystack wasn't what it was supposed to be. A willow thicket was also ingenuously surrounded by hay, then some piled on top, so when the fork was shoved in, it got caught up in a maze of willow whips.

Mike developed the habit now of carrying with him a long prod made from a stick that he used to poke into the haystacks to be certain it actually was a haystack.

Time flew quickly with all the work that needed to be done. There was never any time for leisure. In 1960, they decided to move the cattle herd to the meadow where Louis Dan could look after them again.

It was not an easy drive, as the cows didn't want to leave their familiar range. Amedee had a team and sleigh and was leading his saddle horse. He would go ahead with the team and sleigh and leave it, then go back with his saddle horse and help Mike push the cows up to the sleigh. They repeated this physically draining procedure all the way, back and forth, back and forth. It was late at night when they finally got to Louie's cabin. The dog had worked terribly hard, and was exhausted; so were they. They corralled the cattle, and got out a bottle of whiskey to share with Louie Dan over supper.

Amedee was dead-tired and decided to turn in, and rolled his bedroll out between the wood heater and the door. Louie attempted to stoke up the fire, thinking Amadee would be getting cold by the door. He got the fire going really hot, the stovepipe red all the way up to the roof. As he moved around, he fell onto the hot stovepipe, knocking it down on top of Amadee.

Amadee awoke instantly and jumped up before he got burned. He had been using Mike's mackinaw jacket for a pillow, and it was scorched. There was a lot of pitch in the heater and the cabin quickly filled with black acrid smoke. Mike looked around for Louie but he seemed to have disappeared.

Choking and coughing, Amedee and Mike and one of Louie's sons ran outside to escape the smoke, and there they saw Louie emerging from a different cabin, carrying another stovepipe. Mike tried to follow Louie back inside the cabin to help him get the stovepipe in place, but could not stand the smoke – he had to keep going outside.

For the life of him, he could not understand how Louie could stay in there in that pitch smoke and fasten the stovepipe back together. After things were under control and they could go back inside, Mike asked him how he could stay in there with all that smoke. Louie just laughed and said "that happens a lot, I'm used to it."

Louie Dan was not only used to the smoke – he was used to the country, to the wild horse chases, and he knew how to look after cattle in that unforgiving area.

One time Tuckers and Herricks were up there hunting moose and camped at Louie's for a couple of days. In the evening they were telling stories about how hard it was to pick the low bush blueberries.

Louie listened quietly for awhile, then ventured some advice without any change in expression, "You know how I pick 'em? – I watch a bear eat 'em, when he quits eatin' and ready ta lay down, I shoot 'im, clean 'im out inta the washtub – then I have a washtub fulla blueberries."

Bears were always a topic of interest – most of the cowboys had had at least one encounter with a bear over the space of their many days spent in the bush. Local Tex Fosbery told of an experience in the Upper Nas area when he and the rest of his crew were heading to a camp from Terrace.

As they sped along, a yearling black bear appeared out of nowhere and headed for a spruce tree to climb, unnerved by the foreign intrusion of the truck and its engine.

"Stop, let me out!" yelled Stud (Roy) Graham, an adventurous member of their crew.

The truck rolled to a stop and Stud hurriedly headed to the base of the spruce tree.

As the other men watched in amazement, he started climbing up the tree towards the scrambling bear.

Oblivious to the others in the truck, as they yelled "hey, what're you doing?", Stud continued on with his mission. The cub scratched his way further up the branches, occasionally peering down as Stud steadily shortened the distance between them. The tree was becoming flimsier at the top, and he would soon be trapped, with nowhere else to go.

Suddenly the men in the truck heard a "Yi – ah – you *!*#%$% !" and Stud hastily retreated back down the tree, leaping to hit the ground without taking time to climb down. He stood there shaking his head, and spitting, and started to pull off his shirt. They could see that he was soaking wet, and some yellow kind of liquid was flying off him as he shook his head. The cornered bear had peed all over him.

The desperate bear had used the only defense he had available, and now the other crew members didn't want Stud riding in the truck with them, in his stinky condition. Finally they made him dry himself off with some burlap gunny sacks, and they carried on.

Robin Saunders, a guide and outfitter in the Topley, B.C. area, also experienced the wrath of a black bear. He was surveying some meadow property one warm June morning, when suddenly a noise behind him caught his attention. A black bear, a huge sow, was bounding towards him at a full gallop.

There was no time to get to a tree, even if there had been one. As he desperately glanced around for something, anything, he caught a glimpse of a tiny cub not far behind him. The mother was still coming, and he remembered someone telling him that if you are attacked by a bear or a cougar, you should make yourself look as big and intimidating as possible. The only thing he had seen when he glanced around was a mound of dirt, and he now took an adrenalin-filled flying leap to stand on top of it. Immediately he realized he was ankle-deep in an anthill, as ants by the thousands took defensive action and started climbing up his legs.

The mad mother bear skidded to a halt a mere few yards away. Robin had instinctively drawn the only weapon he had – the pocketknife he always carried. It seemed insignificant in this situation. He turned slowly so as to face her as she circled, her ears flat on her head and her teeth popping in warning. He continued turning to face her, as she was trying to get behind him, and with every turn the infuriated ants attacked him from below. They swarmed over all parts of him, inside his clothing, exploring every inch of his shaking body. Sensing his fear, they were chewing him mercilessly.

It took all his will power not to swat at the ants or rip his clothing off to get rid of them. He used every ounce of stamina to try to talk quietly to the bear, as he had heard that also acts as a confusing tactic. She started to circle again, then suddenly and miraculously slowly began walking away, looking back every few steps.

Robin had just started to relax, still not daring to move, when the mother bear suddenly reconsidered and headed directly back at him again. She covered the distance at an amazing speed and Robin stood absolutely frozen as she stopped a mere yard or so away. This time he didn't look her in the eye, but focussed instead on her body.

Again she left, offering a few huffing noises as she finally broke into a lope and headed to a tree and the cub.

Robin finally relaxed enough to do the fastest job ever of yanking off his clothes. The ants had been savage, his body looked as though he had measles, but he was alive. Shaken and adrenalin-filled, he headed for safer territory.

He felt afterwards that it simply hadn't been his day to die, and he was convinced that if he had turned away from the bear or ran, he would not have survived.

Cattle used to rustle in meadows until after New Years; in one lucky year, until February.

In spring 1955 Mike and Amedee bought 4 Mile Creek Ranch from Edwin (Bumps) Maybee, a potato rancher from Vancouver Island who ended up living in Clinton at the 50 Bar Ranch on Kelly Lake Rd, and eventually moved to Alberta. They began a family operation again – their parents James and Evelyn moved there to help, James was in charge of the irrigating and haying, and young twelve-year-old Frank drove the derrick horse for pulling the loads onto the stacks.

All the while, Mike was trading horses. Money rarely changed hands, it was simply exchanging one deal for another. Mike became masterful at assessing a horse at a glance. The better they bucked, the more he liked it. Jimmy Symes was manager at Diamond S at that time, and Mike did some trading and buying of horses there. He sold some good horses and some bad ones, and he bought some good ones and bad ones. People could not see why he sold his good horses. "If the price is good, anything sells," Mike would say.

"You will never have a good horse that way," someone said. But Mike always had a horse he was happy with.

George Tucker watched a display one day when a five-year-old colt from Art Doubl bucked in the meadow so hard that George remarked "his belly was up to the sky".

Mike also had a red hot team called Babe and Ned; they were spunky, raring to go all the time. They were fed large amounts of grain, and were always ready to run. Mathew Dick borrowed this team one day to go to Scotties Store.

He was back in record time, a big grin on his face – "it's like driving a car, they went so fast!" he remarked.

Work teams having a rest                                    H.Krynen photo

Mike Isnardy, 1947
Isnardy photo

Alice, Jim Holt & Margaret Keefe,
1950s                          Isnardy photo

Amadee Isnardy                          Isnardy photo

# The Wild Horses

## Chapter 16

In the latter part of the 1950's, chasing wild horses was a sporting pastime and a business. So many horses had been turned loose when the tractor and other machinery came in, that the wild herds were becoming a problem, eating up much-needed range, and splitting off into new and faster-growing groups all the time. A bounty of $10.00 was paid by the government for the ears of a wild horse. Some cowboys and ranchers chased the wild horses to corral them, break them, and brand them as their own. Some people, like Harold Engebretson from up along the Fraser River, used to hunt them for meat. There was a market for horse meat at that time.

The wild horses were fast and wily. You needed to be on a horse that could run fast enough to overtake them to rope them or snare them. The pursuers soon learned that they were smart – if you didn't catch one the first time you chased him, you never got another chance, as they would be extra wary the next time.

Mike and Richard Dick were tracking a wild horse through Moose Meadow, Isnardy Meadow and into the Gustafsen Lake area. They had seen this particular horse, and he warranted capturing, as he was fast and cunning. They tracked him through the snow, and eventually came upon the spot where he had spent the night. They could tell by the telltale tracks that showed where he had walked round and round a tall spruce tree all night.

As it was late in the day, they decided to continue this tracking in the light of the next day, and to spend the rest of this day forging a good trail through the deep snow to get back to where they had found his resting place. This would make for much faster travelling the next day.

They were on the trail early the following morning, anxious to use their newly made trail to hopefully overtake the wild horse. They noticed the trail seemed to be even more used, and when they came upon a bright new chocolate bar wrapper lying to one side, their suspicions were confirmed. Someone else had come along, and had the advantage of a nicely packed-down trail to chase their wild horse.

Doggedly, they carried on until they reached the place where the horse had bedded down. Now they could see in the snow where someone had chased this horse, and had given up the chase when the tracks of the wild horse clearly showed that it had actually resorted to hopping – just four holes were left in the snow everytime it had landed, and then hopped again. This left the pursuing horse battling to run through the deep snow, with no hope of catching him.

Mike traded his truck to Jimmy Bulyon for a tall light bay brown stallion called Major. Major had himself been a horse taken from the wild herds. You didn't have to follow the tracks of the wild horses with Major. He would follow them, and always seemed to know where the herds were. Major could be staked out on a rope and, when he sensed the wild horses were nearby, he would pretend that he was going to run with them. He would take off like a bullet, but would stop dead before he got to the end of the rope.

Jimmy Bulyon was a trapper and had ridden out on his trapline in the spring with a bunch of traps, riding Major. The horse bucked him off and he had to walk a long ways home.

Mike ended up using him as his pickup horse at the Riske Creek rodeo, and won the team roping event in the amateur rodeo with him.

Major's reputation grew, and Mike continued using him to rescue bronc riders and bull riders from their wild rides. At the Riske Creek rodeo he watched thoughtfully as he saw that Jimmy had another good bucking horse there, a sorrel that was actually sired by Major in the Whitewater Taseko Lake area. Mike talked to Jimmy for awhile, the result of this conversation was that Mike pulled the saddle off Major, and packed it out of the arena, leading the bucking horse.

Everybody thought he was crazy, trading his quality pickup horse for a bucking horse.

Mike called this horse Whitewater. He worked him in harness for awhile, also bucked with him, and eventually traded him to Jimmy Johnson. Jimmy broke him to ride, and went on a fishing trip with him one day, and claimed that Whitewater tried to throw him in the river. "I better let you have him back, he might kill me!" he announced, as he handed Whitewater back to Mike. This bucking horse was staying.

Many people were out chasing wild horses. Sometimes they worked in groups, running the herds in a certain direction, where others would be lying in wait. One wild horse chaser was Louis Dan, who would hang articles of his clothing on the bushes as he tracked the horses, so the ones following behind would know where the horses crossed. They used to joke that by the end of the day Louis Dan was left with no clothes. Louis was a native from Alkali. He would catch the wild horses – if they were already branded, he would let them go; if they had no brand, he would brand them and let them go. He was selective of the ones he caught – if they had long manes (which would be stuck full of prickly pears), that meant they were too old.

Much horsetrading went on. In 1952 Hank Krynen bought a horse, its home brand was from the west side of the Fraser River. He disappeared from Fox Mountain, where Hank was staying. When Hank asked around if anyone had seen this horse, he was told, "Oh, that horse doesn't like it on that side of the river – he keeps swimming home." All in all, that same horse was probably bought and sold ten times.

Any wild horses that were captured and appeared to have potential were worked with and adopted by the cowboys. Some of them, although broken and trained, never did lose the wildness of spirit they had possessed for so long.

One Sunday at a local rodeo, Ronny Tomlinson was riding one such horse, by the name of Deuce, owned by Tom Desmond. Deuce came barrelling out of the roping chute, never even looked at the calf he was supposed to be chasing, hightailed it to the far end of the arena, jumped the fence and kept on going, with Ronnie on his back, still spiralling his rope overhead in anticipation of launching it towards the calf. After awhile Ronnie came trotting back grinning, waving his hat to the laughter and hooting of all the spectators.

It was about this time, in the midst of a record snowfall and cold spell in 1954, that Amedee had a car accident. He was traveling between the Springhouse School and the guest ranch, when he hit a stump hidden under the snow as he passed Alfred Bowe and Mike in another vehicle. A man by the name of Norton Olsen came along and drove him to the hospital, where injuries to his back and hip were diagnosed. He would be hospitalized for most of the winter.

This unforeseen incident necessitated changes in Mike's plans, as the responsibility for feeding was solely his now. It was a good thing that they had lots of hay, as it was a brutally cold winter, and there were five hundred head to feed, some of them belonging to Mel Moon. The snow was deep, and it was so cold that it was necessary to move the cattle and horses around constantly.

Mike and Jimmy Pigeon decided to ride to Four Mile Pasture to get the yearlings. Above the Chilcotin Bridge at Sheep Creek, they became so cold that they got off to walk for awhile to try and warm up. Jimmy just had a hackamore (a bridle without a bit) on his horse, and nothing around its neck to hold the headstall on. Cold, numb, trudging along with frozen unfeeling fingers and feet, they happened to look back and saw that Jimmy was just dragging an empty hackamore along, no horse. They could see the horse about a quarter of a mile back, grazing by the side of the road.

They laughed all the way back to retrieve the horse, and for many years after.

# Fire on the Meadow

## Chapter 17

**W**ildfires were as much a concern in bygone days as they are now, the difference being there were less fancy homes and buildings to be cindered in those days, and of course little or no insurance. A rancher burnt out then was far more apt to grieve for the loss of precious haystacks or valuable harness, which meant survival for the cattle herd over the long hard winters, than for the loss of a building.

Lightning strikes very often were the start of wildfires. In one warm dry autumn of 1963, the Dog Creek Ranch had been purchased by the ranching Gerry Weingart family from Montana. When they arrived at the Place Ranch, which was part of their purchase, they were disconcerted to find wild horses everywhere on the fields, and fences in major disrepair. As they had hauled thirty-two head of fine Morgan horses all the way from Montana with them, corrals and pens and fences on the fields needed to be put into shape quickly. There were one hundred and thirty cows and calves out in the mountains that had to be gathered before the winter storms hit.

The older cows were as wild as the wild horses and the Weingarts were thankful when good neighbours and local cowboys from the Circle S outfit showed up to help gather in these renegade cattle. One day one of the native cowboys had managed to gather a number of the wild cows, and as they came around a sharp corner on the trail through the thick timber, they met a rider. This was enough to scatter the cows again through the bush on the run. They lost them all, and had to start all over again. There were two sets of cows and calves that they never ever did get to see up close. They waited until after Christmas, when the snow was about a foot deep, then went out to track these animals. It took about four hours before they were able to work them out into a field and finally down the creek towards home. Gerry discovered over the winter that talking to these wild cattle, getting them used to the sound of his voice, did much to settle them down.

Williams Lake saddle-maker Tom Denny occasionally would spend a few days at the Weingart cow camp called Pigeon Creek. They had been out working one day and had decided to ride back to camp, as storm clouds were brewing ominously overhead. They had a small camp stove lit on a wagon, a full one-gallon metal coffee pot brewing away. They poured themselves each a cup of the stout camp-type coffee and sipped away, leaning on the wagon and talking, watching the fast-moving clouds that gathered darkly overhead.

Suddenly a horrific crash and an electrifying flash shook everything – the wagon, the ground, the pot of boiling coffee flew off the stove and sprayed all over them. They fled from the vicinity of the wagon, trying to understand what had happened. They saw then the smoking burning trunk of the old tree that had been standing right beside the wagon.

It had been struck by lightning, which then bolted over and struck the coffee pot. Shaken, they turned their attention to making sure the fire from the strike didn't spread, and thanking their lucky stars that they weren't in the same shape as the tree or the coffee pot.

One of Weingart's valued hired men was Don Thompson, He was a very good worker with machinery, but was not crazy about horses. He had driven a tractor, with a seed drill attached behind, up the south side of Dog Creek to seed some fields. On his way back down the mountain, he put the tractor in low gear on the steep side hill for a slow descent. Following behind him down this hillside was a native driving a team and wagon.

Suddenly something spooked the team and they were running away at top speed, seemingly blind to the tractor and machinery directly in their path. Although the driver was hollering at the top of his lungs, Don heard nothing over the noise of his tractor, and the bumping-along of the seed drill behind. He was oblivious to the approaching pounding hooves, until the whole apparatus caught up to him and the frenzied team attempted to go right over top of the seed drill, the tractor, and of course, the tractor driver. One of the horses managed to jump over top of the seed drill and landed on the tractor right behind Don.

Horses were not his favorite item, and now unbelievably he had one threshing around on his tractor. Leaping off, he took in the rest of the scene in stunned amazement – broken harness, bits and pieces of wagon on his seed drill, and a very excited native trying to gain control of the frothing jittery horses. They finally managed to quiet the horse down enough to get him down off the tractor, and eventually restored some sort of order from the chaos.

Later Don Thompson remarked, "If there ever was a white Indian, there sure was one on that wagon!"

The fall of 1963 was closing the summer off in a succession of warm cloudless days and lengthening cool starstudded nights. Mike Isnardy, as usual, was working with a new horse, a big bay work horse he had bought from Wilfred Pinchbeck. He was a goodlooking horse, well-muscled and quiet, but he had a tendency to quit pulling when the load got heavy, and would allow the other team horse to handle most of the pull alone. When the load was heavy, and the ground was soft, it was important to keep the pulling movement going steadily ahead, as to stop usually meant the wagon or sleigh would sink down and the team may not be able to get it going again. It was never fun to be stuck with a huge load that would than have to be lightened until the horses could move it again.

This horse was annoying Mike so he decided to take a break from his training and check on the hay situation at Paul's Meadow. With the days growing shorter and the honking wedges of wild geese winging steadily southward overhead, all the urgings were there for winter preparation.

He arrived at the meadow and noted there were two large haystacks in the stackyard. He also noticed quite a bit of old hay in places. It was a good day for burning, there was no wind, no rain in sight, and lots of daylight left. Mike decided to set fire to the dry hay late in the afternoon after his other work was done.

Hours later, he returned and started the fire burning and spread it around, pulling the old dry hay into piles as much as possible. For awhile everything went well, then towards evening a gusty wind materialized out of nowhere, and suddenly the fire started to take off. It was burning in a number of areas, and all now started to spread very quickly. Mike at first was running from one spot to another, stomping the flames out with his feet. He saw with horror that the fires were heading straight towards the stackyard and the two precious stacks there.

Mike realized he could not keep up with it. He hesitated for a split second before he ripped off his fairly-new denim jacket, and started to beat at the fire with it. The flames were now not just creeping along the ground, but were reaching high in the air, the small fires had now joined forces into one big fire, igniting grasses and dry shrubs, everything in its path. Maddeningly, when he pounded one burning spot out and moved on to the next, the one he had just put out would flare up again, taunting him. Out of the corner of his eye, he spotted a low muddy spot on the edge of the field. Rushing to it, he threw the now half-burnt jacket into the mud, tramped it in to get it as wet as possible, and flew back to continue beating the flames. That helped a little, but he knew he was still fighting a battle he couldn't possibly win.

Finally he stopped his beating and looked around desperately, knowing he had to get another plan of action in a hurry – the fire had entered the bush and crimson flames were reaching high into the sky as it devoured a thicket of willows. When it finished with the willows, the stackyard would be next.

Mike now ran towards the stacks, and lit more fire, grabbing handfuls of dry hay and grass to get it burning. He made sure he kept it small enough that it couldn't get away from him towards the stacks. He then beat away at the back side of this fire so that it burned towards the other fire, and away from the stackyard.

The big fire crackled its way through the willows towards the stacks, flames licking high in the air. It was

Fire on the Meadow

moving fast, an ominous solid wall of flame that looked like it would not be stopped. It advanced menacingly right up to Mike's little backfire, as he backed off and stood holding his breath to see what would happen.

He knew that if this didn't stop the fire, he had no more moves. He watched in grateful amazement as the huge fire came to the small burned strip, and died out in a matter of seconds. With nothing to feed on, the monster simply quit. There was still fire burning into the underbrush of the willow thicket, and Mike stayed till way past midnight making sure it didn't get past there and go on the attack again.

At long last, Mike breathed a shaky sigh of relief and sank down to the ground with his burnt, muddy jacket in his blackened sooty hands. A beautiful fall day had turned into an exhausting frightening ordeal. His arms ached from pounding at the fire, his boots had holes burned through the soles from stomping on flames, his eyes burned from smoke and ash, he would now have to buy himself a new jacket – he couldn't help but chuckle as he held up the blackened hole-filled mass in front of him. He quietly swore to himself that he would never ever burn another meadow as long as he lived, as he slowly organized himself to head towards home. He looked back a hundred times over his shoulder as he rode away, not trusting the monster to be actually dead.

Later in the fall, Mike met Walter Paul.

"I see where somebody burnt up my meadow, prett' near burnt up yer hay!"

Mike replied, "Yeah, I saw that, too, musta been some hunters."

"Damn fools," said Walter.

Mike was sure the grass grew up sweeter after the meadows burned, as the first place the cows headed to the next spring were the areas that had burned. The grass through the willows grew up bright and green and made great rustling for the cattle.

Walter never did know that Mike had started the fire.

*Fire on the Meadow*

Saddle horses at Pigeon Creek Camp          Weingart photo

Saddlemaker Tom Denny at Pigeon Creek Camp          Weingart photo

# Dentist in a Blizzard

## Chapter 18

L ate that fall in 1963, around the middle of November, Mike moved out to Sticks Meadow and stayed there to sort cattle. One hundred and ninety head were separated off. Matthew helped to move them to Louie Dan's place, and from there Louie Dan drove them to Shorty Meadow. After Christmas, Mike hauled salt with the truck to U.S. Meadow, Louie met him there with the team to haul salt for his bunch of cows.

It was 3:30 a.m. and Mike was out of his bedroll and preparing to get an early start to move twenty-five head to Four Mile Creek that were still at U.S. Meadow. He lit the fire, added more water to the mass of coffee grounds in the blackened metal pot, and set it on the stove to heat. Pulling his boots on and grabbing his jacket, he then headed out to feed the animals. They had twenty miles to go and he had not liked the way the weather was acting the night before.

Lugging the heavy door open, he was immediately engulfed by a white wave of snow. Struggling outside, he looked around in amazement at a quiet heavy world. There was three feet of snow and it was still falling. Shaking off a sticky layer of snow that had already settled on his head, he tramped back into the refuge of the warm cabin and its inviting smell of boiling coffee. As he ate his breakfast, his mind mulled over this new development, and how it would affect his cattle drive. He thought perhaps he could get a bit of a head start if he hurried, and push the cattle to Four Mile before it got any worse. He decided to make haste. He really had no choice, the cattle had to get to the feed.

By daylight he was on his way, pushing the reluctant cattle through deep drifts, which were becoming even deeper at an alarming rate. The thought of the snug little cabin behind him was tantalizing. If only he could light the stove and hunker down in comfort until the storm ran its course. That would definitely have been an option, if it weren't for the cattle, and the precious feed that awaited them at Four Mile.

The cattle weren't exactly co-operative to plough through snow that was banking up to their sides. They balked and turned, attempting to get past Mike back to where they had come from.

"At least the snow isn't crusty" thought Mike. When the snow iced up and got a crust on it, it was necessary to fashion cloth "boots" for the horses out of burlap sacks, and tie them around their fetlocks, as the icy crust cut their feet where they went through. If the snow on top got a hard layer, it really created problems as the cows wouldn't move, and their calves would run on top of it and get away from their mothers.

About half way between Sticks Meadow and Springhouse, at Little Lac La Hache, the situation became quite desperate. The cattle were tired, wet, and were not going to battle their way through any more snowbanks. They stood in exhausted resignation, refusing to move, paying no attention to Mike's prodding and pushing from behind. Not even the border collie nipping and barking at their hind legs could muster them.

Mike climbed down from his black saddle horse, grateful for the huge animal's size and strength. Even in the cold air, enveloped in snow which fell as steadily as though it had life of its own, he was sweating from exertion. Mike now ploughed on foot ahead of the horse, leading him, and then would flounder backwards and forward, making a trail for the cattle. It was like swimming. When he had broken enough of a trail, he whistled for his dog to bring the cattle forward to him, barking and nipping at their heels until they moved ahead. Now they would move for the dog, as a trail was open in front of them.

A good cowdog was as valuable or more so than another cowboy. Without the tireless devoted partnership of his border collie on this particular day, Mike doubted that he would have been able to move these cows.

Progress was slow, and it seemed like an eternity before they finally struggled out to more open ground at Springhouse. The cattle, the dog, and Mike himself all needed to rest, so Mike had coffee with Ward and

Mickey Herrick before setting out again. He was restless to get moving, now that he had a chance to warm up and put his exhaustion out of his mind, to be dealt with later. He had to beat the early darkness. This time he headed out on the main road; without the added effort of having to break trail for the horse and cattle, they made much better time.

Darkness stopped him at Long Lake, at the ranch belonging to George and Elsie Tucker. George, Elsie and Clark Tucker had moved their cattle out to their meadow and weren't home yet because of the snowstorm. Mike put the cattle in a corral and spent the night there, with Verna Tucker and her three small children Connie, Corky and Dolly.

Everyone was battling the snow, and performing desperate feats to keep their animals fed and watered. Hay had to be dug out from under a massive layer of heavy snow, and placed on top of the barns, before it got buried too deep to find. Instead of hauling hay to the animals, stackyard gates were opened up so that the animals had free access to the feed. In the event the men were not able to get to them, they could at least fight their way to the feed.

Mike fell into an immediate exhausted sleep, but was up early next morning, anxious to move these cattle to their destination. He again had to break trail to Bob's Dam, going ahead with the horse and floundering around to make a path for the cows.

It was noon before he got back, so the cattle were by now more rested. After lunch with Verna, he took off again with the cattle. Although Amedee was supposed to meet him at Bob's Dam, there was no sign of him. Mike had half expected this, as it was evident that everyone else was waging the same battle against nature as he was.

Mike pushed the cattle through the gate with a sense of relief, closed it behind them, and returned to Sticks Meadow in the dark. Although he was worrying about his horses left in the meadow with no feed and he was two days late getting back, it didn't take much persuasion for him to stay until the light of day. After

Dentist in a Blizzard

some much needed rest, he pushed himself hard getting back to the horses, then found out he needn't have worried. Herbie Johnny had come along and, seeing the horses had no feed, had opened up the stackyards and let them in to the hay. "Thank heavens I didn't burn up those stacks last fall," Mike thought to himself.

Mike's plan was to move to Moose Meadow behind Lac La Hache. He waited out the snowstorm for two weeks then decided that snow or no snow, he had to go. He took the front bob off the sleigh. The team took two days to break a road through to Tom Felker's above Chimney Lake. There still wasn't much of a trail – he knew he would need a four-horse team to break through to Moose Meadows. Back he went to Springhouse to get another team. He opened the stackyard for the team that he left, they had water as the creek there never did freeze. At Frost Creek he rounded up his team and seventeen horses, and set out again with Moose Meadows as his destination.

This time Richard Dick went along to help him.

Their horse drive got underway, through snowdrifts that had drifted and hardened. Trails were hidden under the snow. Richard chased the horse herd ahead, while Mike came behind with the heavily loaded sleigh, enough food for the winter, plus sacks of necessary grain for the workhorses and saddle horses. Darkness had descended by the time they made it to the slough where George Tucker's son Butch and another boy were feeding the Tucker and Herrick cattle. They were so cold and hungry that they tied the saddle horses and work horses to the trees, and put the rest of the horse herd in an empty stack yard. A good meal in a warm place had never tasted and felt so good. Sleep came instantly.

Before dawn the next morning Mike and Richard left with their saddlehorses to break trail to Moose Meadows, about twenty-five miles away. They traveled one behind the other, every once in a while they would change positions, so that the other one could break trail for awhile. It was brutal work, and exhausting for the lead horse and rider. Upon their arrival, they turned around and went back in the same fashion, this time on the other side, so that they ended up with two tracks broken.

It was around noon by the time they got back to their team, and after eating some lunch, they set off again. Richard chased the horses ahead, and Mike followed behind with the heavy sleigh and the four-horse team. The cumbersome sleigh cut down deep through the snow and got hung up on the big rocks that lay hidden underneath. Twice they had to cut heavy poles that were strong enough to pry the sleigh off the rocks so the exhausted teams could get moving again.

Darkness was stalking them when they finally pulled up in front of the cabin at Moose Meadows. The four horses straining to pull the load were barely moving, just taking jerking steps, they were so tired from the draining journey. They could not have gone another hundred yards.

Mike and Richard were no less exhausted, and they were relieved to see that Matthew had hay put on top of his barn and they were able to feed the horses without having to dig for it, before dragging their weary and frozen bodies into the cabin.

A crackling fire in the cabin, lots of dry wood inside, and a good meal under their belts, they discussed their next step. They still hadn't gotten to the cattle that needed to be fed, and trails that needed to be broken to the stack yard and the place where they were going to feed the cattle. Then the herd had to be brought from Louis Dans to the feeding site at Decker Meadow. The effort needed to keep all these animals alive in these conditions was phenomenal.

At the first hint of daylight, they were out breaking trail to the stackyard with the now rested four-horse team. They forked off a load that would be waiting for the hungry cattle when they got there, then shoveled trails for packing water and cutting wood for the cabin.

Throughout all these exhausting and seemingly endless sojourns through the storms and battling their way through the undone trails, Richard had been complaining about a sore tooth. He was obviously in pain as he tried to maneuver food carefully around his mouth at supper time. He knew he had to get enough food into himself to provide the strength he needed for the grueling trailbreaking and moving of supplies and cattle and horses. Not eating meant becoming weak, and weakness in these situations could be fatal.

Daybreak the following morning found them headed to Louie Dans to get the cattle. The snow was still deep and Richard forged ahead, riding one saddle horse and leading another. When the one he was riding played out, he would take the saddle off him and put it on the other horse, letting the tired horse follow behind on the opened trail for awhile. At lunch time they had progressed as far as Sandy Meadow, where there were some huge spruce trees to sit under out of the snow to have some lunch.

"I wish ya had a pair of pliers, and could pull this blamed tooth out fer me," Richard moaned, holding his jaw in agony. Mike was secretly quite happy that he did not have any pliers with him.

They got ready to leave. There was no time to waste. Mike shoved his hands into the pocket of his big heavy jacket, looking for his gloves. He felt metal handles, and lo' and behold, there were his fencing pliers in his pocket. "Where did they come from?" he couldn't believe they were there, and could not remember putting them in there.

He rather reluctantly pulled the pliers out of his pocket, and without saying a word, held them up for Richard to see. Richard's eyes grew big, and he exclaimed "By God, Mike, pull this tooth out fer me. It's killin' me!"

Mike had done a lot of things, but this was not one of them. "It's too cold, Richard, you're liable to get infection." He really couldn't imagine yanking away at someone's tooth with those pliers – they weren't even all that clean, and the nearest disinfectant was many miles away. God, they didn't even have whiskey to dull the pain.

"Get at 'er!" Richard insisted, opening his mouth wide and pointing to the problem tooth.

Mike realized he was going to have to do this whether he liked it or not. He advanced upon Richard's gaping mouth with the pliers and easily saw the tooth that was causing the problem – a black rotting tooth amid red swollen gums. Richard closed his eyes, locked his mouth opened, and waited trustingly.

Mike got a death-like grip on the pliers and placed them gingerly around the tooth. Richard placed his hand on top of Mike's, to guide him to the exact location of the troublesome molar.

"I'm going to have to do this quickly, " Mike decided. Sending a silent prayer upwards and taking a deep breath, he twisted the pliers around quickly to loosen the tooth, then gave a sharp strong pull. Blood spurted, Richard gave a few muffled grunts, but when Mike looked down at his hand, there was the culprit tooth, bloody and decayed, firmly in the grip of the pliers.

They were out in the snowbound meadow, the restless horses stomping around them, but Richard was grinning happily – "Feels better a'ready ," he said, leaning over the red holes in the snow where he was spitting out blood.

"Keep your tongue on it – don't let it get cold inside," Mike warned him, still worrying about infection. Richard seemed amazingly nonchalant about the entire episode.

Richard decided they had wasted enough valuable time and hurried to mount his horse, his cheek lumpy and swollen, but not in pain anymore. Grinning widely, he said "better git movin ' – we're runnin' outa daylight."

He set out in the lead again, leading a spare horse, Mike following behind. Richard Dick knew this country like the back of his hand, and it was a good thing. He had spent his life trapping and chasing wild horses throughout the entire area, sometimes with his father Mathew Dick or his brother Willard. Theirs was a tough family with ten children, and Richard had spent his entire life travelling and tracking through the entire area, on horseback and on foot. When he was only eight years old, he had saddled up a horse and ridden to the settlement of Williams Lake, as he had never been there. As he rode into the town down the hill from the Dog Creek Road, he noticed a boy about his age by the road, near to where the Canadian Tire Store stands today. This boy had some kind of contraption with big wheels that Richard had never seen before. The boy on his bicycle pedalled up to a fair speed on his bike, then turned some fancy circles on the path.

Richard was mesmerized by this machine, and got down from his horse to have a closer look. He ended up trading his horse and saddle to the boy for the bicycle.

Heading back home, he discovered it wasn't quite as easy as the boy had made it look, riding this wheeled machine. He had to climb back uphill until the Dog Creek Road levelled out on top. By then it had started to rain, and the wheels accumulated a thick layer of clay. He kicked at the wheels to try to dislodge the clogs, but it just filled up again. He fought with it for some distance and finally, totally frustrated, he threw the entire contraption in the bush. He walked all the way home.

Where he and Mike were struggling now with the freight wagon and the four-horse team was rough country, covered with huge rocks. Sometimes there was just enough room between two rocks to get through – if you didn't know just where that avenue was, you could be hung up forever. There were also areas of windfall (downed trees) that would snag up the team and wagon if not avoided. With Richard leading the way through this hazardous minefield, they made it to Shorty Meadow without incident. Mike was now using Richard's knowledge to learn these tricky paths through the boulders and fallen trees. He strived to put to memory the landmarks which indicated where certain obstacles were located under the snow.

There was just an old cabin there at Shorty Meadow, but there was a good spring open for the horses to drink, and feed for them as well.

Shorty Meadow had a tragic past – there had been a murder at the cabin. When the authorities investigated, they were confused to find horse tracks leading to the cabin, but none leaving.

They finally realized the culprit had nailed horse-shoes backwards on his horse's feet, so it would appear that the horse was going in the opposite direction. The tracks that appeared to lead to the cabin were actually heading away.

They put the horses in the corral, and started looking for Louie. No-one was around, and they could see in the snow where Louie had moved the cattle to Cholo Meadow.

They finally caught up to Louie at Cholo Meadow where he was feeding the cattle with two of his boys. They sorted the cattle out, and Mike and Richard took about a hundred and ten head, leaving eighty head with Louie. This way they could make sure they all got enough feed. It was 11 p.m. before they got a chance to have supper, then early the next morning they were ready to head out again. They started to move the hundred and ten cattle from Louie's to Shorty's Meadow, with the help of the two boys. The horses were easy to drive – when they were let out of the corral, they took right off towards Moose Meadows.

The cattle were not to be so easily driven. They didn't want to leave the shelter of the spruce trees at Shorty's Meadow. After many attempts, they finally managed to get them bunched up to the far side of the spruce trees. The tracks left from the horses were frozen, and they were too far apart for the cattle. They did not want to get started.

"Hold them in a bunch and I'll try to get some of them going, "Mike yelled, as he rode right into the cattle and tried to cut a few of them off to get moving. They took off sideways, circling around to join the rest. Mike kept after them, waving and yelling "hi-yi –git going." Finally he managed to isolate three of them and kept them moving in one direction without letting them slip back to the others. He got them on to the horse trail, heading them out briskly so they wouldn't have a chance to turn back. "Bring some more," he yelled to Richard. Richard got about twenty more to follow eventually behind Mike and the three leaders, and then the rest came along with Philip. They could only go single file, so were strung out for miles.

Finally they were back at Sandy Meadow, where Mike had done the tooth extraction on Richard. He was almost afraid to ask Richard if there were any new developments in his mouth. Starving, they dug into the moose meat sandwiches that Louie had prepared, they tasted absolutely delicious. Nothing makes food taste so good as fresh air and hard work.

As they stood around the huge roaring fire, letting their lunch settle, and giving the cattle a chance to rest up for the last leg of the journey to Moose Meadow, Mike again wondered if Richard was going to complain about the gaping hole in his mouth. The only comment that Richard made was that he didn't think they were going to be able to get those cattle moving. After resting for an hour, they headed off again, this time they had no trouble getting the cattle to move, and pulled into Moose Meadow just before dark. The cattle had already been fed, as they had laid out hay for them before they left.

All they had to do was make sure the water hole was open and look after their saddle horses before getting the stove going in the good-sized cabin. Philip Dan stayed the night and headed out the next morning.

Now there was time to settle down. There was no need to be out breaking trail in the pre-dawn darkness, or floundering desperately through snow drifts, or prying the heavy wagon off the rocks. They could relax and see to the feeding of the cattle and horses, keep the wood-stove going, and take time to relax and laugh. Now the tooth-pulling incident was replayed and joked about.

Richard could now take some time for his other past-time of hunting. He went trapping and snaring squirrels and muskrats. He was going to use a horse, but the snow froze so hard that it would cut the horses feet when they broke through. But when the snow was this hard, a person could walk on top without breaking through, and this is what Richard did. He covered miles and miles of countryside on foot.

Mike decided he wanted to go with him on a hunting trip and fed the cattle enough hay to last them for a couple of days. They started out walking, and they walked and walked and walked. Mike was used to riding endless distances on horseback – many times on this walking odyssey he wished for his horse.

Matthew Dick knew his hay, and that good quality hay made the cattle fat, and the horses loved it too. Although they had intentions of chasing wild horses, the hard condition of the snow squelched that idea. So they spent the time trapping and looking after the cattle. Mike, of course, had a few bucking horses along in the herd – Steel Grey, Headache, Witmer Special – he decided to spend time breaking them to ride to give himself something to do through the long snowy winter. Breaking horses was easier in the deep snow. It was harder for the horses to get good traction to buck, and if you did get piled off, it would be into a snowbank.

Amedee got married in this snowdrift winter. Mike was not able to get out to the wedding due to the deep snow and the need to keep the cattle fed.

Tired work team Jumbo and Gumbo at Alkali          Kraynen photo

Cowboys working in winter, Tom Desmond, Ray Johnson, Ray Isnardy
H.Krynen photo

Buckaroos, Tom Carolan and Ralph Van Brunt          Isnardy photo

# The Hanging

## Chapter 19

Mike and Richard were still settled in at Moose Meadow. These were laidback days of seeing to the feeding of the stock, hauling the wood and water in to the cabin, and getting a crackling fire going in the cookstove. The gruelling endurance test of struggling through the blizzard conditions with the cattle, horses, and wagon was already forgotten. The dogs curled up by the stove, content that their masters were not going to be out in the elements, so neither were they. It didn't matter that the snow piled up softly and quietly outside, they knew the spring would come and the green world sleeping beneath would awaken and grow again – along with this would start the calving and haying, and all the hard work that summer brought. Now, and only now, could they take time to relax, tell some jokes, make some bets.

They had a steel crowbar that they used for breaking ice. They decided to hang this crowbar up in the cabin, fastening it to the ceiling. They reasoned they could use this to keep in shape by chinning themselves after supper. One end of the crowbar rested on top of a log of the cabin wall. The top end hung from a rope tied over a log beam. In order for the crowbar to be level, the lower end was closer to the ceiling than the top end.

Mike was outside seeing to the chores one morning, and Richard grabbed this opportunity to hurriedly make a man figure by stuffing straw inside a set of clothing. He fastened the figure all together using a belt, and then hung it by the neck from the crowbar. When he heard Mike coming, he quickly hid behind the door. When Mike pushed the door open, he was startled and fearful to see the body hanging there, legs still swinging a little. It was a few heart-stopping moments before he realized it was just a dummy.

They used the crowbar to keep in shape. They would take turns grabbing the crowbar with their hands, and lifting their bodies up until their chins rested on top of the bar – they would lower themselves, and lift themselves, in a contest with each other as to who could do the most chin-ups before petering out. The more they did, the better they got at doing it, and the competition was getting pretty fierce between them. Fancier maneuvers were needed to better each other. Richard would grab the bar and turn and hang his toes from the bar, lower his head to the floor, then raise himself back up, catching the bar with his hands. He would then let his feet back down to the floor. Try as he might, Mike could never master this feat, he was too long in the body. Richard also started a new chin act – where he would lift himself up, hang his chin over the bar, then release his hands, so that all his weight was held by his chin. To all these antics, Mike would attempt to reciprocate by performing an act more daring and more difficult.

One night Richard was performing this chin act. He pulled himself up and hooked his chin over the bar. This time he was at the end of the bar, where it was very close to the ceiling. The bar was more rigid at this point, there was not so much give to it. He had to turn his head and actually wedge his neck in as it was so close to the ceiling. This way he could brace his head against the ceiling, the bar holding him up by the neck. Mike was lying on the bed with his hands behind his head, watching Richard, and laughing at his antics. Richard had let go of the bar with his hands and hung there. Suddenly he was trying to grab the bar with his hands but could not seem to lift his arms. He began choking and kicking. Mike laughed louder, thinking that on top of everything else, Richard was a pretty damn good actor.

Richard's kicking had been quite desperately violent, and was now losing strength. Mike, still laughing, said "better get down, man, you're going to stretch your neck!"

There was some gurgling and choking and Mike suddenly realized that Richard's hanging body was actually quite still, his arms and legs dangling limply.

*The Hanging*

Looking closer, he saw that Richard's face had turned color, a strange bluish tinge. Jumping to his feet, he rushed over and grabbed Richard's legs, lifting him up to take the pressure off his neck. He got Richard's head out of its hold on the bar, and lifted him down to the floor. Soon normal color began to flow back into his face.

As Richard slowly regained his senses, he looked up at Mike and started to laugh. Although the outcome could have been a lot different, they both knew this would be another incident to look back on and laugh about later.

Mike Isnardy on the trail

Isnardy photo

The Hanging

A typical cow camp cabin

Cows had to be tough to survive

They say there's a special horse for every cowboy, and a special cowboy for every horse. Roger Dickson at Springhouse had bought a sorrel standardbred horse from Heine Zirnhelt, by the name of Rusty. Rusty was a handsome steed, some sixteen hands high, a three-year old with a white blaze on his face and two white hind feet. Mike watched with interest as Roger rode Rusty around. He was a good roping horse. He was snorty and held his head high, he seemed proud of himself. He was from old stock raised on the Douglas Lake Ranch, with a previous reputation for bucking.

One day when Mike was working at the cattle sale, Roger asked him if he would ride Rusty as he worked at the auction.

"I don't like riding someone else's horse," replied Mike. He had been to many auctions and indoor events, and knew that some animals, horses and cows alike, could be unpredictable with the noise of a crowd and unfamiliar environment. He had seen some real wrecks in an arena, and at the back of his mind was the thought of possibly injuring or crippling someone else's horse.

Roger was insistent and, after being asked two or three more times, Mike happily agreed. He liked the way this horse moved, and the attitude he expressed.

Every week on his way to the cattle sale, Mike would stop by Roger's place and load Rusty into his truck, and the two of them would head off to work as partners at the sale. In time, it seemed that Rusty was as anxious to go as Mike was to take him.

This went on for some time until one day Roger said, "Mike, you may as well take Rusty home with you to use on the Ranch, as well as at the sale. This would save you having to stop in here and pick him up every week."

After carrying on in this fashion for awhile, Roger asked Mike how he liked Rusty. By this time, Mike and Rusty had formed a firm relationship. Roger said, "Why don't you trade me three yearling heifers for that horse?"

Without hesitation, Mike replied, "Okay, it's a deal!" And a deal it was, and one that neither Mike nor Rusty ever regretted.

Mike gave Rusty the respect and care he deserved; in return Rusty became the best assistant he had ever had. He would do anything for Mike – he worked cattle, was a good roping horse, and had good speed and attention. Mike used him as a pick-up horse at rodeos, calf-roping, hazing for bulldoggers, hazing for the girl's undecorating. When working with cattle in a corral, Rusty would cut the cattle out by himself, and never seemed to play out or get winded. He seemed to love his job.

Rusty shared the passion that Mike had for the wild horses. He loved to head out with Mike on the trail of the wild horses through all kinds of timber, and was fast enough to not only get Mike close enough to throw a rope, but to actually get alongside the fleeing cayuses, so Mike could simply drop a loop over their heads. Whether it was a wild horse on the end of the rope, or a rodeo bull, Rusty had no trouble digging his feet in and holding on as whatever it was on the other end strained and dove and fought to get free.

Rusty never bucked with Mike on his back, but Mike chuckled on numerous occasions when he saw Rusty throw off other cowboys who borrowed him from time to time.

He was a one-man horse. Mike used Rusty for a long time, until he got old and stiff and ready for retirement in the meadows. Then Mike went looking for a replacement, and never again saw or found another horse like Rusty.

Many of the cowboys had a special relationship with some certain horse that was suited to them and to no-one else. Hank Krynen traded his truck to Tommy Desmond for a horse called Jack, who remained his lead horse and partner for twenty-five years.

Amedee had a favorite horse called Trigger, and Richard Dick had a perfect partnership with a horse called Bull Hornet, that Mike had bought for $60.00.

Lenny DeRose acquired a rather ugly big bay horse from the Circle S Ranch. He wasn't pretty – he had a big head and had the habit of letting his lower lip hang down, causing Lenny to endure a fair bit of ribbing over Old Nevada. He didn't care. He had learned a secret about Nevada. He had discovered that the reason Old Nevada bucked everyone else off but him was that he didn't like the reins lifted up. Lenny left the reins down, and Old Nevada never bucked with him. He was a fast walker, and would pull with all his heart when an animal was on the end of the rider's rope. He loved to head cattle, and would actually knock other horses out of the way to head a cow.

Mike was on a continual quest for horses. It was like an addiction. He travelled to Oregon with George and Elsie Tucker, where they came back with two stallions they purchased from a horse breeder by the name of Bill Lootin. George had bought a palomino yearling stallion by the name of Dusty Deuce. Mike hadn't planned on buying any horses, but ended up buying a two-year-old coal-black stallion named Crack-time, from the same mare, but a different sire, a stallion called Nut Cracker.

Mike had quite a time persuading the border authorities to allow him to bring Crack Time over the border, as he had not specified on the way down that he was bringing a horse back. Finally they agreed to allow Mike and the stallion across the border, Mike paying double what he had planned.

It was a long hard trip for the horses. They tired from standing and needed to be allowed out of the horse trailer periodically. When they arrived in Vancouver, they rented a motel, careful to pick one that was in a location where they could sneak the horses out of the trailer for some exercise, feed and water. They then tied them to the horse trailer. They would get up early and load the horses and be gone before anyone could complain to them about the telltale horse signs of manure and hay left behind.

They then drove as far as Cache Creek, and repeated this procedure. They got the horses home in this fashion, none the worse for wear, and Mike started working with Crackers. Although he had lots of speed for chasing wild horses, Mike was disappointed to learn that he had no cow sense whatsoever, and had to be shown over and over what to do. He eventually got swamp fever, and had to be put down.

Mike frequented horse sales. George Tucker had heard about a quarter horse sale in Spokane, Washington, and they drove down in Mike's one-ton truck, with plans to bring the truck back full of horses. To their consternation, the horses they picked out the day before the sale as being what they wanted, were bid up to very high prices. Mike ended up buying a "cheap" quarterhorse mare that he had not looked at before, for $1800.00. She was carrying a foal though, from a good stallion, so he reasoned he was actually getting two horses for that price.

This time they had no trouble at the border, did their usual early flight from the motel, and got the horse home in fine shape. Mike cared for her over the winter and, in the spring, decided to move her over to his Dad's place, where there were no other horses to bother her at foaling time. It was a good move, as James was tickled to have the new foal, a little filly sorrel called Shotsie. He fooled around with her all the time, so that soon she was following him around everywhere.

The next year Mike took the mare to Cherry Creek Ranch by Kamloops to be bred again. She ended up losing this foal before it was born. They tried to breed her again. This time they called in Dr. Greenaway, the veterinarian in Kamloops, who claimed she was "windsucked" and although she was in foal again, he could not guarantee that it would be successful. True to this, she again lost her foal before delivery. Now Mike had to look seriously at what it was costing to get more foals from this mare. Vet fees, room and board, stud fees, travel costs, all added up to over $1000.00 now, and there was no guarantee that things would be different in the future.

The following year, he left her in the pasture with a stud, but he never did get another foal from her. He did not enjoy riding her. She was muscle-bound, and did not have a good "traveling gait". Riding a horse with a choppy gait like that was tiring, and when Mike knew he was going to be riding all day, he would choose instead

Rusty

some tried and true horse, or one that came from the wild herds in the reserve pastures.

Mike had also learned a valuable lesson – that high-cost horses, registered with papers and fancy names, did not guarantee good results.

Everybody at home gave Mike a hard time whenever he returned from a trip, as it was a well-known fact that he could not go anywhere without coming home with at least one more horse.

Mike hadn't realized what a treasure he had had in Rusty until he tried to replace him.

BUCKING BRONCOS arrived in Prince George from Williams Lake last Wednesday afternoon for the annual Fall Fair beginning August 17 at Willowvale Ranch. Riding the lead horse is Mike Isnardy, of Spring House, where the horses came from. They were corailed on an island near Shelley before being brought back to the hub city for the fair. About 250 entrants are expected. Williams Lake girl, Cathy Sutherland, has been named queen of the Little Britches Rodeo, that is to run at the same time.

(Prince George Citizen Photo)

*Mike and a remuda of horses*          *Prince George Citizen photo*

*Rusty*

Mike Isnardy, pickup man for Gil Bowe          H. Krynen photo

Alkali horses at Big Swamp          H. Krynen photo

# The Rodeo Begins

## Chapter 21

Amedee's marriage brought changes. Now he had reason to stick around home at Four Mile. Mike was at Springhouse, carrying on the work there. It was an adjustment to make for both of them, as they had hayed together and played together for many years, they always had someone to share the various jobs. It didn't seem the same, not having each other handy – they were both used to working together. Gradually a natural split came to make more sense of the workload. They agreed to split the cattle herd and the machinery, and each go on their own – Amedee at Four Mile, and Mike at Springhouse.

Lee Skipp, a lawyer in Williams Lake, was called upon to draw up the papers, and they were legally on their own, for the first time.

Mike found himself hiring a man to fill in the empty spot left by Amedee, and Richard Dick came to work. Mike knew him to be a reliable man, someone he could count on to be able to do just about anything that was required, whether it be to climb on a wild horse, or a broken-down tractor, or a chainsaw, or calving heifers – there was no job he didn't take on. Mike watched him get on a horse called Kapoos once, that bucked and bucked. It seemed like the horse's belly was going up to the sky, but Richard hung on like a prickly pear cactus. There was an occasional good drunk shared with him, where they laughed until they cried, telling tales of various horses and the trials of riding them, roping them, being made fools of, and their conquests.

Every fall Richard Dick's dad starting guiding on hunting trips, and Richard packed up and went with him. Mike knew better than to try to stop him or entice him to stay. This was usually at the time when Mike was ready to ship cattle, and it was difficult to round up and sort the cattle without Richard's help for when Elton Elliot's cattle-liner arrived.

In the spring, Mike found the haying situation such

that he had run out of hay at Springhouse and was forced to calve the cows out in the meadow. There was no real setup for calving, no barn, no straw, and the snow stayed late. This caused a chain reaction of cows not having enough milk for the calves, the calves becoming weak and succumbing to scours and other illnesses.

As soon as a calf was born, Mike would carry it into the cabin, as that was the only dry place. When it was dry and steady on its feet, with a good start of milk in its belly, he would take it back out to the mother. Pretty soon the cabin was so full of calves that Mike nearly had to move out, there was barely room for him. Although he was alone, Mathew Dick's family were only about five miles away, and he knew he could always get help there if he really needed it. He waited anxiously for the spring to sprout some lush green grass, and as Four Mile Creek range was along the river, it was the first to "green up" in the spring.

Mike moved the cattle there. Richard and Steve Johnson helped with the drive. The calves were small, and tired easily. They ended up leaving quite a few cow-calf pairs along the way to follow along at their own speed. Although they did lose a few calves in the meadow that spring, the move to the warmer river range improved their health. After they rested up from their trip to get there, they bounced around with their tails in the air.

The cattle herd had grown, they had a 90% calf crop from Dan Lee's cows. At branding time, half of these belonged to the A&P for looking after the cows. Dan Lee would brand one, then A&P would brand one, until all the calves were done.

Having finally gotten the smell, sight, and feel of potatoes out of his system, Mike could now concentrate on working with what he loved best – horses. While he was at the A&P, he had acquired some horses to work with – he purchased three horses from Tom Carlin at Frost Creek for $75.00. One was a 1200lb. grey gelding. Duke Martin and his wife from the C1 Ranch met Mike riding in the field one day. After giving Mike the news that the Ford garage in Williams Lake had burnt down,

Duke wanted to buy that horse from Mike, but he wouldn't sell.

He also got a small palomino from Ray Pigeon called Meano; and a brown mare from Alex Milliken at Four Mile Creek. Mike had a keen eye for horseflesh, and was always on the lookout for a special animal. His practiced eye now fell on a little bay gelding called Kentucky, and he bought him from Pascal Bates. Kentucky had come originally from Bert Johnson at Alkali Lake and had never been broke.

A young man by the name of Lyle Linns hauled in a load of hay one night, unhooked his team, and was watering them at the well. Mike had been working with Kentucky and also led him to the well for a drink. They discussed Kentucky's merits.

"If you can ride him back to the barn, you can have him," Mike jokingly said.

"O.K!" Lyle was quick to take up the challenge, and handed the lines of his team to Mike to hold.

Kentucky only had a halter on, and Lyle jumped confidently on his back bareback.

Kentucky lit off bucking, throwing Lyle headfirst into a snowbank. Mike still had his horse.

The more Mike worked with Kentucky, the better he got. He had a few habits. He had been chased so much that he had never gotten over it – if he was ever chased, he lit out as far and as fast as he could go. Mike took him to the Springhouse Roping Club, which had sprung up naturally just from everyone getting together with their animals, to have a weekend workout.

Kentucky was eventually sold to Tom Denny.

Mike built a log enclosure five feet high to make it easier to train and work with the wild horses and young green colts. This was a natural place for everyone to gather to practice some calf-roping. Every Sunday some of the local boys would show up to practice their roping skills on the calves and against each other. Some could only spare enough time to come after supper, and Mike himself could not always find the time. If Mike was busy elsewhere, whoever came would round up some cows and calves and carry on their roping on their own.

The Springhouse Roping Club evolved from a few serious cowboys getting together on Sunday afternoons at Mike's place to practice roping, work with their horses, compare techniques, and basically just have some good-natured competition. More and more people started to show up.

Everyone looked forward to Sunday afternoons when they could work their horses and pit their skills against each other. Much horse trading and swapping was done.

Gradually it expanded, as more and more needed equipment and pens appeared. Gil Bowe built a calf chute, with an open end, for the calf-roping event. Mike had built a chute for vaccinating cows. This was a special chute that opened sideways into the arena, and it wasn't long before the calf-roping cowboys suggested that this would be a perfect chute for horses – and they could also sharpen their bronc-riding skills. Mike always had horses handy, and now whole-heartedly began gathering horses that he knew would buck.

Mike loved buying rodeo horses. He could oftentimes negotiate a real steal of a deal, because the horses he was buying were usually ones that the owners couldn't handle and didn't want. He wanted horses that had a bad reputation. It didn't matter if they were stonecold ugly, in fact that was a bonus – big jugheads, big feet, tangled bramble tails, the wilder they looked made them seem even more ornery and intimidating. He was looking for strength, endurance and attitude.

Not only did they need pens and corrals and chutes, there were special riggings needed for the different events, and it seemed that everyone had something to contribute. Someone produced a worn bronc saddle. A bronc saddle differs from a normal roping saddle in that it has no dangerous saddle horn to cause harm to the rider. They also needed halters and ropes for the bucking horses, and a flank strap with two rings that could be tightened up on the horse's flanks to encourage bucking. Someone else magically produced a bareback rigging. This was really not a saddle at all, but a small back pad with two cinches and a leather strap to tighten it around the horse's belly, and a leather strap with hand holds in place of a saddle horn. Out of nowhere someone produced a bull rope – for wild cow and bull riding, a rope was tied around the flank with a bell to goad the animal into bucking.

To further the bull-riding event, Mike now brought twelve to fifteen two-year-old bulls from Garry Hook in Kamloops.

So started the Springhouse Rodeo. It was a little sluggish – there was only one chute – so only one horse or one cow could be used at a time. While some calf -ropers were roping, someone else would be getting a bronc or a cow ready for riding. More and more people started coming, from further and further away. Enthusiasm was contagious, and it was not too long before four chutes were built. There was much laughter, much jesting and betting, a great camaraderie amongst these tough ranchers and cowboys as they let off some steam and took a day off from the neverending ranching duties at their respective homesteads. Competition grew keener, and rules were put into place to keep everything fair.

Mike found himself right smack in the middle of an escalating business. Rodeos were popular, and word was getting around that his string of bucking horses and other stock were next to none. He found himself hauling his stock all the way from Terrace in the far north, to Courtenay and Port Alberni on the southern coast, and all the interior towns in between that welcomed the popular rodeo events.

The Springhouse Rodeo was fast becoming a flourishing enterprise. Admission was charged at the gate, to cover some of the expenses. Competitors threw money into a pot for prize money for the winners. Pretty soon Bert Roberts volunteered to be announcer, and a P.A. system was rigged up. There were no bleachers – people lined up on the fence to watch and cheer and to sometimes bail off when one of the bucking frothing animals came too near to the spot they were sitting.

Saddle bronc riding, bareback riding, cow riding, team roping, calf roping, wild cow milking, a wild horse race, barrel racing, stake racing, bull riding – the rodeo grew and flourished from the seeds of collective camaraderie and competitive spirit.

This brought together people from all over – Clinton, Cache Creek, Meldrum Creek, Riske Creek, Big Creek, Anaheim, as far away as Quesnel, Horsefly, and the Chilcotin, even from Ft. St. John, far to the north. Cowboys and their families appeared like magic out of the bush to try their skills against the reigning winners, to show off their well-trained roping horses, and cowdogs. People put more care and training into their horses, as they wanted to shine in the competition, and certainly didn't want the embarrassment of a disobedient horse in front of the crowd.

They camped out near the rodeo grounds area. These people were always hungry, so it was inevitable that the next thing to materialize was a concession stand selling hot dogs and drinks. The Springhouse Womens Institute took over this welcome addition to the rodeo.

"Hell, Mike, you have everything you need here for rodeoing – why don't you start contracting rodeos?" Gil Bowe asked Mike one day, as the trucks were loading up the horses after yet another Sunday afternoon exhibition.

A man by the name of Harold Hartley from Quesnel had been attending Mike's rodeos at Springhouse and knew the caliber of bucking horses that were there. Mike soon found himself putting on his first rodeo at Bouchie Lake just out of Quesnel. Joe Seebol, a friend of Mike's who was one of the first Greyhound bus drivers and had originally lived in Williams Lake, now had a hotel in Quesnel, and all the rodeo draws were done the night before the rodeo in the "office" at the hotel. Harold Hartley, George Henigar, Bruce Fosbery started as the Committee, and over the years the setup grew. Now Mike's friend Elton Elliot hauled the horses to the rodeos, in two trucks and trailers.

Mike's bucking horse string grew and the number of rodeo demands grew. He took his string to Williams Lake to the outdoor arena, then to the Trailriders arena in the early spring; west to Riske Creek; pretty soon north to McLeese Lake. After four rodeos at McLeese

Lake, they realized the crowds were not big enough to make it pay. Mike travelled next to Terrace, far to the north, where a rodeo was a novelty and a huge success.

Mike's bucking stock string – the Double G – was famous and became known to rodeo and ranching communities everywhere. Remnants of this bucking string are still bucking today, that all started out at Mike's backyard as a few cowboying and ranching friends having some Sunday afternoon fun. Stories of spectacular rides and special horses will never die, with the old familiar names spoken with reverence and admiration.

Thus the first organized rodeo association in BC was born and nurtured along by Mike, his long-time friend Willie Crosina, Bert Roberts, Bill Twan, and many others. It was named the IARA (Interior Amateur Rodeo Association). It developed into the IRA, and finally became what is known as the BCRA (British Columbia Rodeo Association) today. It became evident that a rodeo was an event that brought people out in droves. They loved watching the cowboys and cowgirls pit their strengths and wits against the bucking and fleeing animals.

Willie Crosina developed a rodeo clown act with his partner, a donkey called Bimbo. The crowd loved their crazy antics, and it always pleased Willie to be able to make people laugh. At the same time, he made sure the thrown cowboys didn't get into trouble with the bucking horses and bulls. In later years, Willie would be the proud recipient of the Overlander Lifetime Achievement Award for Outstanding Dedication to the Sport of Rodeo.

The cowboys made and kept many good memories from the rodeos and stampedes. Hermie Maurice sold a three-year-old colt to Hank Krynen. When he hadn't yet chosen a name for the young horse, Buck Mammel laughingly offered "Why don't you call him Bloomers?" Everyone within earshot hooted with glee, and of course Bloomers was stuck with that name from that time on. Hank endured much ribbing about his horse with the crazy name.

At the Williams Lake Stampede, the local huge rodeo gathering, a prize was given for the "Best Dressed Cowboy" as everyone turned out in their finest clothes for the rodeo. This event was now taking place in the ring.

Hank was busy getting ready for the calf-roping event that he had entered. The problem he had was that he couldn't find his horse Bloomers anywhere. Suddenly over the loudspeaker, he heard Clarence Bryson's voice boom out, "and now for the Best-dressed Horse ..." followed by an uproar of laughter.

Heading towards the ring, he couldn't figure out why Tommy Desmond was bringing Bloomers directly in front of the grandstand, parading him around. Worse than that, the crowd was laughing and pointing hysterically.

Finally Tommy Desmond turned Bloomers around so Hank could see the backside of the horse. Chrissy Pigeon had sewn a huge pair of bloomers and they had fitted them over the legs and hind end of Hank's horse. A sign that read "Best Dressed Horse" was hung over Bloomer's rump.

Mortified, Hank could only watch helplessly as Bloomers paraded around the ring in her big pink bloomers.

The Roman Race was a particular favorite at certain rodeos, a daring event which consisted of a rider standing atop two horses, one foot on the back of each horse. The well-trained horses had to run in absolute sync with each other, so as not to unbalance their daring rider. Local Bill Twan, cowboss for the Alkali Lake Ranch outfit, was well-known in this race, balancing atop his two well-matched white horses Penny and Lucky.

Time might dim the memory of who the riders were, but the bucking horses will never be forgotten – the cowboys would remember the "money makers" from Mike Isnardy's bucking string - those who would give them a good ride for the best dollars –

Whitewater, Steel Grey, Empty Saddle, Wild Bill, Silver Tip, Rough Cut, a tricky blue-grey horse called Zombie, twisting horses Hard Twist and Mr. Twister, a strong bay called Payday, a wild bareback horse called Big Enough, Hungry Henry, Phantom Lady, Pelican, a strong chestnut called Cream of the Cariboo, Spider, Jalopy, Dark Hawk, and a whitefaced buckskin called Jigsaw, lightfooted Grasshopper, Snowflake, Perfection,

Deception, Lady Luck, Alkali Special, Dog Creek Special, Colonel Blue (a big iron-gray blue roan who would take a run and then dive), Snip, Centennial, Badger Mountain, Blue Cross, a bay mare called Hot Seat who was seldom ridden, Old Daddy, Tucker Special, Oregon Pete, Smoky, Black Magic, a blue roan called Blue Jeans, Bay Banner, Dark Cloud, Grey Ghost, Two Spot, Papoose, a pinto called War Paint, New Deal, Jake, Campfire – were just a few of the ever-growing bucking string. The riders came to know the horses and their respective traits and quirks. They tried to outthink them and outsmart them and outmaneuver them.

And then there was the grand-daddy of all bucking horses, the famous and unforgettable Ol' Come-Apart.

Bill Twan, ready for the Roman Race
Ken Hauff photo

The Rodeo Begins

Mike Isnardy, Springhouse Rodeo, 1966                    H. Krynen photo

Bernard Dick                                            H. Krynen photo

# Ol' Come-Apart

## Chapter 22

Of all the bucking horses that twisted and gyrated and pounded their way around the rodeo rings, one stood out far above the others. A few days before Christmas in the winter of 1970, Andy Chelsea happened to run into Mike. He claimed he had a horse that he had been trying to break, and the horse simply would not be tamed. Mike's ears perked up like radar – he knew that if Andy Chelsea couldn't break a horse, this was definitely an animal he wanted to see. Andy Chelsea was Pat Chelsea's son; they came from down around Gang Ranch way, and were historically great horsemen.

After some haggling and horsetrading, Mike bought this horse from Andy Chelsea for $75.00 and decided to leave him down at the River Range for the winter, and pick him up in the spring.

When he brought the horse home in the spring, he realized he had a great rodeo horse. Mike's bucking horse string was well-known by now as excellent performers and Harold Hartley, the head man for the rodeos, attended even the Springhouse Rodeo and promoted these bucking horses as of superior quality. These weren't old plough horses trained to kick up their heels and hop around – they were spirited performers hand-picked by Mike from all over the place, and he definitely had an eye for ones that would put on a worthwhile show.

His new bucking horse was not all that big – an average sized bay with a white face. He didn't really catch attention until someone got on his back, and the chute door swung open.

Then this horse, soon called "Ol' Come-Apart" would literally come unglued. He would go to any length to unseat a rider, never turning the way they expected him to, sometimes seeming to almost turn inside out if he had to. Broncbuster after hopeful broncbuster tried to ride him – they would study his moves and think they had him figured out, then find themselves face down with a mouthful of rodeo dirt. His reputation grew and grew. Over the expanse of his lifetime of bucking, only three cowboys were able to stay on him for the required eight seconds. One of these successful riders was Jack Palmantier from out west of Williams Lake. A broncrider from Smithers, Robert Bowers, tore his glove right in half while attempting to stay on his back. Ol' Come-Apart just simply bucked hard and fast and seriously until the rider was gone.

A ride on Ol' Come-Apart was entertaining from start to finish. All the broncriders wanted to draw him for a ride at first; the marks would be high, and they knew what their status would be in the rodeo world if they were lucky enough to stay on for an interminable eight seconds.

It wasn't long before the broncriders all feared drawing his name.

Ol' Come-Apart seemed to have a personal issue with anyone who climbed on his back. It became necessary to blindfold him in the chute before the gate opened, as he would buck and rear so hard before the gate opened that the rider wouldn't be able to get on.

He was solid and strong. Local wellknown broncrider Sonny DeRose established a record for himself of being able to ride most bucking horses and, after a few attempts to ride Ol' Come-Apart, never ever wanted to get on him again.

Wherever Ol' Come-Apart was featured at a rodeo, the arena or bleachers were packed. It was this horse they came to see and applaud. People even climbed trees in order to see him, when Mike trucked his rodeo string all the way to Terrace in northern B.C. The rodeo crowds in the northern towns were very enthusiastic fans, as a rodeo wasn't something they had access to very often.

Mike continued on his quest for good bucking horses – he never stopped looking and listening, and "putting out feelers". The first thing he wanted to know about anyone new he met, was what kind of horse they rode. He bought, sold and traded all manner of hopeful buckers, including five four-year-old colts from Circle S Ranch when Jimmy Syme was manager.

*Ol' Come-Apart*

He eventually sold his ranch to Clark and Verna Tucker, and moved in with his long-time friends Terry and Willie Crosina. He and his friend Frank Overton still worked at the stockyards from time to time, and he still enjoyed being pick-up man at the rodeos every chance he got.

Nothing he ever bought or traded or raised even came close to breaking the astounding record of throw-offs that Ol' Come-Apart held. In the sport of rodeo, Ol' Come-Apart was a top-notch athlete.

Ol' Come-Apart eventually ended up in the U.S. after a sale price of $7000.00 U.S. Rumor filtered back to the Cariboo that the top-listed bronc rider in the U.S. had attempted to ride him, and this experience caused him to stop broncriding altogether.

Ol' Come-Apart had left the country, but his name is still spoken today with reverence by every rodeo participant and fan in the province of British Columbia.

Ol' Come Apart, rider Sonny DeRose          Patrick Hattenberger photo

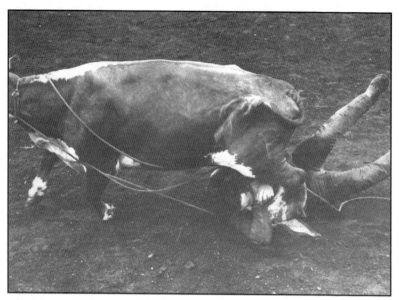

Jim Pigeon, wild cow milking

Krynen photo

Hank Krynen roping from Skeezik

# The Accident

## Chapter 23

C hristmas crept in on quiet snowy feet in 1975. A comfortable peace settled into the community as everyone enjoyed the rarity of a day away from routine, anticipating the inevitable feast that would materialize before the day was over.

Mike was spending a leisurely Christmas Day with Terry and Willy Crosina, and he and Willy were in high spirits as they left the house to do the morning feeding. Christmas Day was no different than any other day when it came to making sure the animals were looked after.

Mike's truck was piled with hay bales right to the top of the stock racks. Willy climbed in behind the wheel and maneuvered the truck near to the wagon that was going to haul the load out to the milling cattle herd. Mike climbed to the top of the bales in preparation to throw them down to the wagon.

"Good thing you're climbing up there before you get plumb full of turkey," Willy remarked.

"Right," laughed Mike, "it might be tough tomorrow!" With that he grabbed at the first heavy bale, to jerk it up in the air and throw down to Willy waiting to stack them on the wagon.

He had performed this action hundreds upon hundreds of times in his lifetime.

On this particular day, in this fate-stricken second in time, the string broke in his hands, and he flew off the truck, landing on his head, towards the back of his neck, on the frozen ground.

What followed was a succession of horror-stricken realizations for Willy, as Mike had landed a mere three feet from him from such a high distance. Willy was familiar with First Aid, and knew that he must not allow Mike to move at all, for fear of spinal cord or neck injury.

"Stay still!!" he yelled at the crumpled figure that was now attempting to start getting up.

"I'm alright," came a shaky reply from Mike.

"Don't move!!" Willy yelled again – he knew his toughest job would be to keep his ever-active friend from injuring himself further. Mike was lying partially on one side, and Willy now jumped behind him and braced his knees against Mike's back for support. "Now stay still, don't move at all," he again implored.

He glanced across the yard towards the house, and was relieved to see his son coming down the steps.

"Call an ambulance," he yelled, "and bring some quilts!" His son hesitated a mere second before realizing something desperate had happened, then quickly disappeared into the house. Almost immediately he reappeared on the run, racing towards the immobile pair on the ground, an armful of blankets flapping in his arms.

"Mom's calling the ambulance," he offered breathlessly, as he and Willy very gently and carefully propped Mike's neck and head, and surrounded him with a quilt to keep warm. Although it wasn't a severely cold Christmas Day, Mike was lying in the snow.

"I think I can get up," Mike muttered, gingerly trying to flex his fingers and move his legs.

"Oh no you don't," repeated Willy, bracing his knees tighter against Mike's back, "Stay where you are!"

"My arms and legs are tingling," Mike insisted, "I probably just need to get up and move a bit."

Willy staunchly refused Mike's ambitions to get up and shake off his injuries, as he always had in the past.

Although it seemed like an eternity, an ambulance materialized up the roadway in record time, within a half hour. Willy's son had run out to the main road and watched for them, leading them to the bundled forms on the ground without delay.

Two ambulance attendants, Jim Gibson and his partner, Bob, carefully stabilized Mike, carrying on the same "don't move" orders that Willy had maintained. Finally, they closed the back doors of the ambulance, with Mike securely fastened to a gurney inside, and headed off for the hospital.

The Crosina family stood quietly by and watched morosely as the ambulance disappeared down the driveway, their Christmas plans suddenly in a shambles.

Mike at first waited for the feeling in his numbed

body to return. He was certain that with some time to heal, everything would be back to normal. It was inconceivable to him to think that it wouldn't. He patiently endured what seemed an endless routine of poking, prodding, x-rays and testing, confident that someone soon would tell him to take it easy, get some rest, and he would soon be on his feet again.

From Williams Lake Hospital, he was flown to Shaughnessy Hospital in Vancouver, where a grim diagnosis of "spinal cord injury due to a broken neck" was finally gently but firmly given to him by the specialists there who had pored over his x-rays, hoping to find something other than what they were seeing.

There was no kind way of delivering this message. Mike was introduced to life in a wheelchair, and transferred to G.F. Strong Hospital for rehabilitation and therapy.

This seemed an unthinkable transition for someone as active, healthy, strong and capable as Mike Isnardy had been his entire life. He had survived horrific falls from bucking horses, crazy accidents with runaway teams and machinery, blizzards, nearly drowning in a frozen lake, and now a two-second fall would dictate how he would spend the rest of his days.

It was as though Someone had watched Mike overcome every obstacle in his life with such ease, and decided to plant a huge mountain now in his path, just to see if and how he would negotiate his way around it.

Although Mike's initial inner reactions were of shock and rejection to his new circumstances, his very strong spirit remained undaunted. Although he outwardly portrayed the inner strength all who knew him were accustomed to, he secretly harboured a disbelief that his injuries were permanent. His concern and respect for his family and friends buoyed him up, as he sensed their devastation and sorrow. They surrounded him with their love and support, trying to keep up his spirits, then wept at their own helplessness when they were out of his sight.

Literally everything Mike did now presented a challenge. It took extreme effort and learned procedure to accomplish what had come naturally and

The Accident

automatically to him before. It was discouraging, and sometimes dark despair took over, but not for long.

Little by little, step by painful step, he succumbed to the realization that waiting for the day when he would wake up and be able to feel his lower extremities was a futile pastime. He finally understood that day was not going to materialize.

With this realization came acceptance. With acceptance came a concerted effort to make the most of what he was left with. It was like harnessing together another team of work horses – his mind and the physical assets he still owned. He forced his mind to concentrate on what he could do, not what he couldn't. And he called upon the sheer physical strength of the upper body that he still possessed, to work together with his mind to perform what his entire body had done before December 25, 1975.

Mike was fiercely independent, as was apparent by the semi-solitary way of life he was accustomed to living. He had spent his life in the company of the wild things of the bush, natural elements of weather, skies, sunsets and sunrises. To be confined indoors, for the first time in his life subjected to the downright frightening world he discovered inside the television set, was a situation he didn't tolerate for very long. And he was absolutely determined never to become a burden to anyone. His friends and family discovered they could not do things for him. He would learn to do everything himself – somehow.

As soon as was humanly possible, Mike purchased a customized vehicle, especially designed to lift his wheelchair into place, with hand controls for driving. Then it became everyone's concern to find him, as he explored every back road and trail he could find. They worried about him getting stuck, or falling out of his chair and not being able to get back in. He probably did all these things, but somehow found a solution to every problem he encountered.

Mike lived with his lifelong friends Terry and Willie Crosina for some time, before moving to Riske Creek to live with his brother Ken. He eventually bought a house in the

*The Accident*

Glendale area of Williams Lake, where his next-door neighbours Pat and Linda Seary, became valuable friends.

Here Mike exercised his independence. He looked after all his own needs, including growing a garden. He attended every rodeo and horse event that came along, his good nature and every prevalent sense of humor endeared him to all who came to know him. He absolutely refused to entertain any notions of self-pity for the cruel cards that life had dealt him.

At the Williams Lake Stampede in 2002, Mike Isnardy was overcome with emotion when he was inducted into the Cowboy Hall of Fame. Never was there one so deserving, and he was greatly honored to see his face and name alongside the other cowboys whom he had spent his lifetime respecting and idolizing.

And what of that formidable mountain that was totally blocking Mike's pathway?

Well, he simply climbed it steadily and laboriously to its summit, and firmly planted his flag right on the very top. Then he laughed all the way down the other side.

Mike Isnardy receiving Cowboy Hall of Fame award
(Mike Puhallo standing)

The Accident

# Epilogue

Mike Isnardy passed away peacefully in his sleep

At 1:02 a.m. Tuesday, November 30, 2004

photo from "Chute that Horse" courtesy of Mike Isnardy

# Gang Ranch the Real Story
## by Judy Alsager

The Gang Ranch – British Columbia's sprawling and legendary million-acre cattle empire at long last came under Canadian ownership in 1978. Judy Alsager, one of the owners, takes us on a sincere and moving journey of breathtaking scenic images through the tumultuous times that see the Ranch rise proudly from its previous comatose state to once again become a thriving exciting operation. She shares with us the heartache and desperation of the Alsager family as a bizarre series of events brings the Gang Ranch toppling down without warning, thrusting them into an alien labyrinth of what actually transpired to tear the Alsager family apart, and how the Gang Ranch was wrested away from this family's grasp, resulting in the tragic loss of one of Canada's grandest and historical assets.

Judy Alsager now lives upriver from the Gang Ranch on her 130-acre farm on the banks of the Fraser River, halfway between Williams Lake and Quesnel. She has survived ten years of court battles and bankruptcies, a divorce, raising her four children, and never once looked back on her association with the Gang Ranch with regret.

The book is $17.95 plus g.s.t. and is available on line from the Blue Door Publishing company website: www.caribooginseng.com telephone/fax: 250-747-8402

# Coqualeetza, No Backward Step
## by Dorothy McIvor

**Article from The Williams Lake Tribune, Feb 15, 2002**

Dorothy McIvor was tired of hearing all the bad things about residential schools. So, well into her 80s, she decided to write a book in praise of a residential school. Residential schools for native children have become notorious for being places where children were abused, so it is a rare book published in praise of one of these schools.

Local author Judy Alsager was instrumental in having the book published. Judy edited Dorothy's notes and pulled the book together for her, then had it published by her own Blue Door Publishing company. Judy came to learn about Dorothy through her Marguerite neighbour Kim McIvor, who is Dorothy's granddaughter.

The book is $16.95 plus g.s.t. and is available on line from the Blue Door Publishing company website: www.caribooginseng.com telephone/fax: 250-747-8402